Ladies Who Lunch

By the same authors

Your Secret Servant

Ann Reed and Marilyn Pfaltz

Illustrations by Annette Kossen

LADIES WHO LUNCH

Charles Scribner's Sons   New York

A - 9.72 (H)

Printed in the United States of America
Library of Congress Catalog Card Number 72-1212
SBN 684-12947-7 (cloth)

Dedicated to the patience and fortitude
of those who aided and supported our
testing and tasting.

Contents

Foreword

Reading cookbooks is a caloryless experience for many. But it may be impossible to keep the pleasures vicarious while perusing *Ladies Who Lunch*.

Except for those with unshakable will power, the desire to rush to the kitchen and start cooking will be overwhelming.

Marilyn Pfaltz and Ann Reed have put together a tempting collection of recipes that should inspire a lot of lunching. Advance preparation is the key to the "helpless" household and the authors have written the recipes so the minimum amount of last minute work is required; some can be completely prepared ahead of time.

I hope the title of the book will not discourage seekers after good recipes who never give lunches for ladies—or anyone else for that matter.

There are many excellent dishes that would be equally as appropriate for dinner parties or those marvelously relaxing weekend lunches when husbands join their wives.

September 1972   MARIAN BURROS

Marian Burros is Food Editor of *The Washington Evening Star* and *Daily News* and co-author of numerous cookbooks, among them *Elegant but Easy Cookbook* and most recently *The Summertime Cookbook*.

Introduction

"Come to lunch" is a familiar phrase in every woman's world, whether formally inscribed on paper or breezily issued by phone. In today's whirl, a few hours of relaxation and enjoyment in the company of friends over a delicious lunch are especially treasured. In the contemporary cooking scene of convenience foods and packaged meals, noontime elegance is a special treat for guests. A guest who has rushed through her household chores in order to relax at lunch does not expect to be met by a frantic hostess. Therefore create an atmosphere of charm and graciousness by having all details done before the doorbell rings. Many of the recipes can be frozen, and almost all of them can be prepared in advance. Fix everything the day before and be your own guest.

For elegant entertaining arrange a beautiful table with your best china and a simple or elaborate arrangement of fruits or flowers. Everything served should be fussed over to look its delectable best. Serve ladylike portions. Lunch will then be a delight instead of a regret for having eaten too much. Remember, too, guests are a captive audience. Don't indulge in French fried octopus unless you are sure they are either game to try anything or familiar enough to ask for an omelet.

Two technical notes: The recipes generally serve six. They are easy to double when serving six to twelve people. The leftovers aren't bad either! Secondly, all oven temperatures and baking times are subject to the idiosyncrasies of individual ovens. An oven thermometer is a good idea.

The complicated ways of yeast, the time-consuming preparations of soups from scratch, and the intricate motions of special desserts are ignored and left for the cooking schools to explain. This collection of recipes for LADIES WHO LUNCH are all easy to prepare and elegant to serve. Best of all they are spectacularly delicious to taste.

Menu suggestions

COLD WEATHER

Crabmeat and Mushroom Casserole   (p. 66)
Waldorf Salad Mold   (p. 105)
Cheese Popovers   (p. 38)
Ambrosia   (p. 131)

Eggs Mornay   (p. 45)
Fresh Tomato and Rice Salad   (p. 110)
Bacon Muffins   (p. 31)
Apricot Chiffon Pie   (p. 129)

Ham Timbales with Mushroom Sauce   (p. 94)
Western Salad   (p. 116)
Corn Bread   (p. 33)
Strawberry Meringue   (p. 164)

Parsley Soup   (p. 17)
Russian Meat Pie   (p. 88)
Beet and Egg Salad   (p. 104)
Brown Sugar Custard   (p. 136)

Chicken Soufflé   (p. 78)
Spinach Salad   (p. 113)
Butter Pecan Circles   (p. 28)
Sherry-Almond Chiffon Pie   (p. 162)

Fresh Mushroom Soup   (p. 16)
Easy Shrimp Newburg   (p. 60)
Gazpacho Salad Mold   (p. 112)
Pecan Pie   (p. 157)

Moussaka   (p. 86)
Orange Cheese Salad Bowl   (p. 108)
Sesame Seed Sticks   (p. 35)
Toasted Almond-Orange Mousse   (p. 130)

Clam Bisque   (p. 12)
Mushrooms Stuffed with Chicken Livers in Wine Sauce   (p. 80)
Grapefruit-Apple Mold   (p. 106)
Rum Devil's Food Cake   (p. 163)

HOT WEATHER

Carrot Vichyssoise   (p. 4)
Melon and Cold Meat Platter   (p. 89)
Sour Cream and Chive Biscuits   (p. 36)
Pecan Ice Cream Balls   (p. 150)

Chilled Spinach Soup   (p. 8)
Chicken Salad Mandalay   (p. 80)
Date-Nut Muffins   (p. 31)
Coffee Mousse   (p. 140)

Avocado Soup   (p. 2)
Crabmeat Mousse   (p. 65)
Bacon and Lettuce Salad   (p. 102)
Orange Biscuits   (p. 36)
Chilled Cantaloupe and Blueberries   (p. 132)

Nicoise Salad   (p. 70)
Beth's Pumpkin Bread   (p. 32)
Coconut Lemon Chiffon Dessert   (p. 143)

Jellied Tarragon Broth   (p. 5)
Curried Chicken Salad with Fruit   (p. 75)
Banana Muffins   (p. 31)
Frozen Ginger Roll   (p. 146)

Watermelon Basket   (p. 84)
Ruby Salad Dressing   (p. 119)
Spice Bread   (p. 27)
Eggnog Chiffon Pie   (p. 156)

Sour Cream Tomato Soup   (p. 9)
Shrimp and Avocado Salad   (p. 115)
Scones   (p. 34)
Peach Macaroon Freeze   (p. 161)

Tomato Aspic Carousel   (p. 84)
Apple-Cheese-Nut Bread   (p. 22)
Chocolate Torte   (p. 137)

INFORMAL

Onion Soup.   (p. 12)
Devonshire Sandwiches   (p. 82)
Ginger Pear Salad   (p. 105)
Layered Apricot Bars   (p. 128)

Tuna Fish Spaghetti Salad   (p. 71)
Pineapple and Walnut Bread   (p. 29)
Stewed Rhubarb and Strawberries   (p. 135)

Eggplant and Clam Casserole   (p. 70)
Grapefruit-Apple Mold   (p. 106)
Chocolate Macaroons   (p. 138)

Mushroom Roll   (p. 50)
Garden Vegetable Mold   (p. 117)
Marbled Cream Cheese Brownies   (p. 154)

Orange Chef's Salad   (p. 76)
Pinwheel Onion Rolls   (p. 34)
Mocha-Nut Pie   (p. 156)

Chicken Sandwich Soufflé   (p. 79)
Cantaloupe and Cucumber Salad   (p. 107)
Cream Velvet Freeze   (p. 164)

Salmon Loaf   (p. 62)
Spinach Salad   (p. 113)
Caraway Bread   (p. 27)
Lemon Pie   (p. 139)

Chicken-Sausage-Mushroom Pie   (p. 77)
Bing Cherry Salad   (p. 101)
Chocolate Nut Crunch   (p. 138)

FORMAL

Clear Mushroom Soup   (p. 10)
Coquilles St. Jacques   (p. 69)
Molded Tomato Salad   (p. 114)
Parmesan Cheese Wafers   (p. 31)
Chocolate Pot de Crème   (p. 137)

Chicken and Sour Cream Mousse   (p. 76)
Avocado Salad   (p. 108)
Lemon Bread   (p. 23)
Frozen Cherry Jubilee Pie   (p. 133)

Gazpacho #2   (p. 6)
Shrimp with Béarnaise Sauce   (p. 61)
Broccoli Mousse   (p. 103)
Herb Sticks   (p. 30)
Bananes Flambées   (p. 135)

Cream of Water Cress Soup   (p. 16)
Crêpes with Salmon Filling   (p. 49)
Sweet and Sour Lettuce   (p. 117)
Baked Orange Alaska   (p. 151)

Veal and Ham Rolls   (p. 89)
Cheese Aspic with Curry Dressing   (p. 104)
Nut Bread   (p. 26)
Brandied Peach with Vanilla Sauce   (p. 160)

Almond Soup   (p. 15)
Mushroom-Stuffed Chicken Breasts   (p. 78)
Cranberry Horseradish Mousse   (p. 103)
Never-Fall Popovers   (p. 33)
Berries with Wine Sauce   (p. 142)

Cream of Green Bean Soup   (p. 13)
Shrimp Strudel   (p. 59)
Endive and Grapefruit   (p. 101)
Melba Toast   (p. 21)
Cocoa-Filled Angel Food   (p. 142)

Chilled Curried Chicken Soup   (p. 5)
Wild Rice Mold with Shrimp   (p. 57)
Orange-and-Onion Salad   (p. 112)
Cold Fudge Soufflé   (p. 146)

Soups

With a blender on the counter and chicken broth in the pantry or on the stove, anybody can be the best soup-maker in the neighborhood. A soup stockpot constantly simmering on the back burner is described in books, but rarely found in modern kitchens. The availability of a wide range of canned or prepared stock has transformed soup-making from a lengthy procedure of boiling, clarifying, thickening and seasoning into a simple method of combining prepared bases with desired flavors.

Exotic soup names should not intimidate any cook. After all, the famous Crème Vichyssoise invented by the master chef Louis Diat is nothing more than his French mother's leek-and-potato soup named after his home town of Vichy, France. All kinds of soups of international origins and intriguing names have been Americanized for ease of preparation. Spanish gazpacho, Russian borscht and Scandinavian fruit soups are all fixed in a very few minutes in the blender.

1

Soup is a versatile part of a luncheon menu. A light, cold jellied soup or clear consommé may introduce the main course, or a shell-fish bisque or vegetable cream soup may be served as the entrée. A delicious hot or cold soup served with salad and bread is welcomed in the calorie-conscious world of LADIES WHO LUNCH. Soup always seems less filling and fattening than meat or fish. A quart of soup makes about six servings. Double the recipe if the soup is to be served as an entrée.

Cold soups should be thoroughly cooled and served in well-chilled bowls. A quick way to chill the soup is to place it in the freezer before serving. Hot soups should be served in lidded or well-heated dishes. The touch of elegance to the soup bowl is the garnish. Where possible, identify the taste of the soup by garnishing appropriately—chopped peanuts for peanut soup, bits of cress for water cress soup or toasted pumpkin seeds for pumpkin soup. Garnishes should attract the eye and appeal to the taste. Chopped chives, cucumber, celery, tomato and croutons are a few suggestions.

With a little imagination and a nice sounding home town, you might even make an original culinary creation!

AVOCADO SOUP
Blender

2	small avocados
1½	cups chicken broth
3/4	cup sour cream
3/4	cup light cream
1	tsp onion juice
	salt and freshly ground black pepper to taste
1	tbsp lemon juice
	Garnish: lemon and paprika

Peel avocados and dice. Place all ingredients in a blender and mix until thoroughly puréed. Chill soup in tightly covered jar in refrigerator. Serve cold garnished with thin slices of lemon and paprika. Avocado will darken within 2 hr. of preparation. Serves 6.

QUICK BORSCHT
Blender

1	can (No. 2) beets, sliced (2½ cups)
1	can (10½-oz) consommé
1	can (10½-oz) cream of celery soup
1	tsp horseradish
1/2	tsp garlic powder
	Garnish: sour cream, fresh tarragon or parsley

Place beets and half the beet liquid in blender. Add remaining ingredients and blend until smooth. Chill at least 3 hr. Serve garnished with a dollop of sour cream and a pinch of chopped tarragon or parsley. Serves 6.

COLD BLUEBERRY SOUP

2	pkg (10-oz) frozen blueberries, thawed
1	cup water
3	tbsp sugar
1	tsp cinnamon
2/3	cup sour cream
	Garnish: lemon

Combine blueberries, water, sugar and cinnamon. Bring to a boil and stir until sugar is dissolved. Press through a sieve. Stir 1/2 cup of blueberry purée into the sour cream. Then slowly stir in the rest. Chill for several hours. Serve in chilled cups and garnish with lemon slices. Serves 6.

CARROT VICHYSSOISE
Blender

    2   tbsp butter
    5   scallions, diced
    1   can (13¾-oz) chicken broth (1¾ cups)
    2   cups cooked carrots, diced
 1/2   tsp salt
        dash of pepper
    1   tbsp dry sherry
 1/2   cup light cream
        Garnish: water cress leaves

Melt butter and sauté scallions until transparent. Add 1 cup of chicken broth. Cover and simmer for 10 min. Place broth mixture, remaining broth, carrots, salt and pepper in blender. Blend until smooth. Add sherry and cream and chill thoroughly. Serve garnished with water cress leaves. Serves 6.

CREAM OF LIMA BEAN SOUP
Blender

    2   tbsp butter
    1   bunch scallions, chopped
    1   pkg (10-oz) frozen baby lima beans, cooked and drained
 1/4   tsp salt
 1/8   tsp pepper
 1/2   tsp marjoram
    4   sprigs chopped parsley
    1   can (13¾-oz) chicken broth (1¾ cups)
 3/4   cup light cream
        Garnish: chives or parsley

Melt butter in saucepan and sauté scallions. Place scallions and lima beans in blender. Add salt, pepper, marjoram and parsley. Cover and blend until smooth. Leaving the motor on, remove cover and add the chicken broth and then, gradually, the cream. Blend 5 sec. longer. Chill. Serve very cold garnished with chopped chives or parsley. Serves 6.

CHILLED CURRIED CHICKEN SOUP

1½	tbsp butter
1	large onion, sliced
3	apples, peeled, cored and sliced
1½	tbsp flour
3	tsp curry powder
	salt and pepper to taste
	dash of cayenne pepper
1½	cans (13¾-oz) chicken broth (about 2¾ cups)
3/4	cup dry sherry
3/4	cup cooked chicken, diced
1½	cups light cream
	Garnish: apple

Melt butter and sauté onions and apples until onions are transparent. Mix flour with curry, salt, pepper and cayenne. Stir into apple mixture and cook slowly for about 3 min. Add broth gradually, stirring constantly. Add wine and simmer for 10 min., stirring often. Press through a fine sieve. Add chicken pieces and cream. Chill. Serve in small chilled bowls and garnish with unpeeled apple bits. Serves 6.

JELLIED TARRAGON BROTH

3	cans (13¾-oz) chicken broth (5¼ cups)
3	tsp tarragon
1	tbsp unflavored gelatin
1/4	cup cold water
	Garnish: lemon or lime and parsley or chives

Simmer chicken broth for about 5 min. Add tarragon. Soften gelatin in 1/4 cup cold water for about 5 min. Add to hot broth and stir until gelatin is dissolved. Refrigerate about 4 hr. Skim off any fat that has formed on the top. Serve cold garnished with slices of lemon or lime and chopped parsley or chives. Serves 6–8.

GAZPACHO #1
Blender

1	clove of garlic
1	medium onion
1	cucumber, peeled
3	tomatoes, peeled
1	green pepper, seeded
4	eggs, beaten
1/4	tsp salt
	dash of cayenne pepper
1/4	cup vinegar
1/4	cup olive oil
3/4	cup tomato juice

Garnish: tomato, onion, cucumber, celery, green pepper

Cut up vegetables and place all ingredients in blender and mix until thoroughly puréed. Chill overnight to allow flavors to blend. Serve in well-chilled bowls. Garnishes such as chopped tomato, onion, cucumber, celery and green pepper can be served in separate dishes for the guests' own selection. Serves 6.

GAZPACHO #2
Blender

1	clove of garlic
2	cans (8-oz) tomato sauce
1	can (10-oz) beef consommé
1/4	cup vinegar
1/3	cup salad oil
1/4	tsp Tabasco sauce
1	medium onion
1	medium cucumber, peeled
2	medium tomatoes, peeled
1	small green pepper, seeded
	salt and pepper to taste

Garnish: tomato, cucumber, green pepper, onion

Rub inside of a 2-qt. jar with cut side of garlic clove. Pour tomato sauce, consommé, vinegar, oil, and Tabasco into a blender. Blend until mixed. Pour about two-thirds of this mixture into the prepared jar. Cut up vegetables and add to the remaining liquid in the blender. Blend on low speed just until vegetables are finely chopped. Pour into jar. Season with salt and pepper. Serve very cold garnished with additional chopped vegetables. Flavors blend best when soup is chilled overnight. Serves 6.

VICHYSSOISE
Blender

3	tbsp butter
3	leeks or green onions, sliced
1	medium onion, sliced
4	medium potatoes, thinly sliced
1½	cans (13¾-oz) chicken broth (2½ cups)
2	tsp salt
2	cups milk
1/2	tsp grated nutmeg
1½	cups heavy cream
	Garnish: chives

Melt butter and sauté the leeks and onions until transparent. Add potatoes, chicken broth and salt. Simmer for 30 min. or until potatoes are tender. Pour the mixture into a blender and purée. Return the mixture to the pan, adding milk, nutmeg and cream and bring to a boil. Return to blender and blend until smooth. Refrigerate. Serve in chilled cups and garnish with chopped chives. This soup must be served very cold. It may be put into the freezing compartment of your refrigerator about 1 hr. before serving. Serves 6–8.

CHILLED SPINACH SOUP
Blender

1/4	cup butter
1/4	cup flour
1/2	can (13¾-oz) chicken broth (1 cup)
1	cup milk
1	pkg (10-oz) frozen chopped spinach, cooked and drained
1	tbsp lemon juice
	salt and pepper to taste
2	tbsp dry sherry
1/2	cup heavy cream, whipped
	Garnish: 1 hard-boiled egg

Melt butter and stir in flour until well blended. Gradually add chicken broth and milk, stirring constantly. Cook, stirring, over low heat until soup is thickened and smooth. Add spinach, lemon juice, salt and pepper. Simmer over low heat for 2–3 min. longer. Add sherry. Chill thoroughly. To serve: stir whipped cream into soup. Garnish with circle of egg white and finely sieved egg yolk. Serve in small chilled cups. Serves 6.

FRESH TOMATO CREAM SOUP
Blender

3	cups fresh, ripe tomatoes, chopped
1½	cups light cream
4	tsp chopped parsley
4	tsp basil
1½	tbsp ketchup
1½	tsp salt
	Garnish: lemon

Place all ingredients in blender and mix until thoroughly puréed. Chill. Serve in chilled bowls garnished with lemon slices. Serves 6.

SOUR CREAM TOMATO SOUP

2	cans (1-lb) tomatoes
1	bunch scallions, minced
1	tsp salt
1	tsp sugar
	pepper to taste
1/2	tsp thyme
1/4	tsp marjoram
2	tsp curry powder
2	tsp grated lemon rind
	juice of 1 medium lemon
1	cup sour cream
	Garnish: parsley

Press tomatoes and juice through coarse sieve. Add all other ingredients to tomato except sour cream. Mix and chill for at least 2 hr. for flavors to blend. Strain again. Fold in sour cream. Serve very cold garnished with chopped parsley. Serves 6.

TOMATO JUICE SOUP

4	cups tomato juice
1	can (13¾-oz) beef broth (1¾ cups)
4	whole cloves
1	small onion, sliced
1	bay leaf
	freshly grated black pepper to taste
1/2	tsp basil
1	tsp sugar
1–2	tbsp lemon juice
	Garnish: croutons or popcorn

Combine all ingredients except lemon juice in a saucepan. Cover and simmer for 20 min. Strain soup and add lemon juice. To serve: reheat and garnish with the croutons or popcorn. Serves 6.

CRAB BISQUE

Blender

       4   cups water
       4   medium potatoes, peeled and quartered
       2   medium onions, sliced
     1/2   bay leaf
       1   tsp tarragon
     1/2   tsp thyme
     1/2   tsp garlic powder
       2   tsp salt
       1   pkg (6-oz) frozen crabmeat, thawed, drained and
           flaked
       1   can (13¾-oz) chicken broth (1¾ cups)
           pepper to taste
       2   egg yolks
     1/2   cup heavy cream
     1/4   cup white wine

Bring 2 cups water to a boil. Add potatoes, onions, bay leaf, tarragon, thyme, garlic powder and salt. Cover and simmer until vegetables are tender. Add crabmeat and remove bay leaf. Pour into blender and purée. Return this mixture to saucepan and add broth and remaining 2 cups water. Bring to a boil. Remove from heat and stir in egg yolks which have been beaten with the cream. Add the wine. Serve hot or very cold garnished with paprika. Lobster or shrimp may be used instead of crabmeat. Serves 8–10.

CLEAR MUSHROOM SOUP

     3/4   lb fresh mushrooms, minced
       3   cans (13¾-oz) beef broth (5¼ cups)
           salt and pepper to taste
       1   tsp basil
       2   tbsp dry white wine

Combine mushrooms and beef broth. Add salt, pepper and basil and simmer for about 20 min. To serve: stir in the wine and serve very hot. Serves 6–8.

TUNA BISQUE

    1   can (10¾-oz) cream of mushroom soup
    1   can (10¾-oz) cream of asparagus soup
1½   soup cans milk
1/2   cup light cream
    1   can (7-oz) tuna fish, drained and flaked
1/4   cup dry sherry
        Garnish: heavy cream, chives

Combine soups. Stir in milk and cream. Heat, stirring constantly. Add tuna and sherry. Serve hot with a dollop of whipped cream and a sprinkling of chopped chives. Serves 6–8.

CREAM OF CAULIFLOWER SOUP
Blender

    1   pkg (10-oz) frozen cauliflower
1/4   cup butter
    2   tbsp chopped onion
    3   celery ribs, minced
1/4   cup flour
    2   cans (13¾-oz) chicken broth (3½ cups)
1½   cups milk
    1   egg yolk, beaten
1/2   cup light cream
    1   tsp basil
    1   tsp chopped parsley
        salt, pepper and nutmeg to taste
        Garnish: grated American cheese

Cook cauliflower according to package directions. Pour cooking liquid and cauliflower into blender and purée. Melt butter and sauté onion and celery until onion is transparent. Add flour and stir until well blended. Gradually add broth, stirring until thickened and smooth. Combine milk, egg yolk, cream and seasonings. Add to broth mixture. Add puréed cauliflower. Heat slowly. Serve garnished with grated cheese. Serves 6–8.

CLAM BISQUE
Blender

   6 tbsp butter
   1 large onion, chopped
   6 tbsp flour
   2 cans (10-oz) minced clams
   2 cups clam juice
   3 cups light cream
   3 tbsp tomato paste
   3 tbsp lemon juice
      Garnish: parsley

Melt butter and sauté onion until transparent. Stir in flour until well blended. Add clams and their liquid and clam juice. Cook, stirring, until mixture thickens. Simmer about 15 min. to blend flavors. Pour into blender and blend until smooth. Return to saucepan. Mix cream, tomato paste and lemon juice together. Stir into soup. Serve hot and garnish with chopped parsley. Serves 8.

ONION SOUP

   1/2 cup butter
     3 cups sliced onions
     3 cans (13¾-oz) chicken broth (5¼ cups)
   1½   cups water
     3 envelopes instant beef broth mix
   1/2 tsp gravy seasoning
        salt and pepper to taste
     6 slices of French bread, toasted
   3/4 cup freshly grated Parmesan cheese

Preheat oven to 400°.
Melt 6 tbsp. butter and sauté onions until they are transparent. Add the broth, water, instant broth mix and gravy seasoning. Simmer for 15 min. Season with salt and pepper. To serve: place the toast in a 2-qt. casserole or in individual onion soup dishes, add the soup and sprinkle with the cheese. Dot with remaining butter. Bake about 10 min. or until top is brown. Serves 8–10.

CREAM OF GREEN BEAN SOUP
Blender

       2 tbsp butter
       2 tbsp flour
     1/2 tsp salt
          pepper to taste
       2 cups milk
     1/4 tsp nutmeg
       2 pkg (10-oz) frozen green beans, cooked and drained
       3 cups heavy cream
       2 tbsp Cognac
          Garnish: parsley and chives

Melt butter and stir in flour, salt and pepper until well blended. Gradually add milk and nutmeg, stirring constantly until sauce is thickened and smooth. Add beans and simmer for 5 min. Purée the mixture in blender. Combine purée with heavy cream and heat, but do not boil. To serve: add Cognac and garnish with chopped parsley and chives. Serves 6.

WILLIAMSBURG PEANUT SOUP

       4 tbsp butter
     1/2 cup diced celery
       1 small onion, minced
    1½   tbsp flour
       1 can (13¾-oz) chicken broth (1¾ cups)
     1/2 cup creamy-style peanut butter
     1/2 cup light cream
          Garnish: parsley and peanuts

Melt butter and sauté celery and onion until onion is transparent. Stir in flour and mix until smooth. Gradually add chicken broth and bring to a boil, stirring often. Add peanut butter and simmer for 20 min., stirring frequently. To serve: stir in cream and heat. Garnish with chopped parsley and peanuts. Serves: 8–10.

FLORIDA SOUP

2   cans (10½-oz) tomato soup
2/3   cups fresh orange juice
     salt and pepper to taste
     Garnish: orange

Combine tomato soup and orange juice. Season with salt and pepper. Chill. Serve very cold garnished with orange slices. Serves 6.

PUMPKIN SOUP

2   tbsp butter
2   tbsp minced onion
2   tbsp flour
1/2   tsp paprika
1/4   tsp nutmeg
1   can (13¾-oz) chicken broth (1¾ cups)
2   cups milk
1   cup cooked pumpkin
1   egg yolk
1   cup heavy cream
2–3   tbsp dry sherry

Garnish: toasted pumpkin seeds

Melt butter and sauté onion until transparent. Blend in flour, paprika and nutmeg. Gradually add chicken broth and milk. Cook, stirring, until soup thickens and comes to a boil. Stir in the pumpkin and transfer the soup to the top of a double boiler. Cook over water for about 25 min. Beat egg yolk with heavy cream in a bowl. Gradually beat a small amount of the hot soup into the egg mixture and pour back into the remaining soup. Stir in sherry. Serve either hot or thoroughly chilled garnished with toasted pumpkin seed. Serves 6.

CURRIED ASPARAGUS SOUP

1/4 cup butter
2 tbsp grated onion
2–3 tsp curry powder
1 can (13¾-oz) chicken broth (1¾ cups)
2 cans (10½-oz) cream of asparagus soup
1 cup milk
1 cup light cream
3 egg yolks, beaten
1/4 cup dry sherry
Garnish: large avocado

Melt butter and sauté onion with curry powder until onion is transparent. Add chicken broth and simmer 20 min. Combine asparagus soup, milk, cream and egg yolks. Add to broth. Heat, stirring, just to simmer and add sherry. This soup will curdle if heated too much. If this happens, it may be put in blender for 5 sec. To serve: peel and dice avocado. Garnish the soup with avocado pieces. Serves 6.

ALMOND SOUP

2 tbsp butter, softened
2 tbsp cornstarch
3 cans (13¾-oz) chicken broth (5¼ cups)
1 cup heavy cream
1 cup finely chopped almonds
2 tbsp finely chopped water cress leaves
salt and pepper to taste

Blend butter and cornstarch together until smooth. Heat chicken broth and gradually stir into the butter mixture. Simmer soup for about 5 min., stirring often. Remove from heat and add cream and almonds. Allow to stand for at least 30 min. for flavors to blend. To serve: reheat the soup, add water cress leaves and season with salt and pepper. Serves 6.

CREAM OF WATER CRESS SOUP
Blender

        1   can (13¾-oz) chicken broth (1¾ cups)
       20   tender water cress stems
        3   tbsp cornstarch
        1   cup heavy cream
            salt and pepper to taste
        1   tsp lemon juice
        2   tbsp butter
            Garnish: water cress leaves

Reserve 6 tbsp. of chicken broth. Place the remainder in a saucepan and add the water cress stems. Bring to a boil and simmer for about 5 min. Mix cornstarch with 6 tbsp. of cold chicken broth and stir into the simmering broth mixture. Remove from heat and pour into blender. Purée until smooth. Return soup to saucepan, add cream, salt and pepper and bring soup to a boil, stirring often. Remove from heat and add lemon juice and butter. Serve hot garnished with water cress leaves. Serves 6.

FRESH MUSHROOM SOUP

        6   tbsp butter
        1   medium onion, chopped
      1/2   lb fresh mushrooms, chopped
        4   tbsp flour
        1   envelope instant beef broth mix
        2   cans (13¾-oz) beef broth (3¾ cups)
        1   bay leaf
            freshly ground black pepper to taste
      3/4   cup light cream
            Garnish: parsley

Melt butter and sauté onion and mushroom until onion is transparent. Remove from heat and stir in flour and instant broth mix until blended. Gradually add beef broth, stirring constantly. Add bay leaf and pepper. Simmer for 5 min. Remove bay leaf. To serve:

add the cream and heat, but do not boil. Garnish with chopped parsley. Serves 6.

PARSLEY SOUP
Blender

      1   large onion, chopped
      1   tbsp olive oil
      2   cups parsley leaves
    2½   cans (13¾-oz) chicken broth (4¼ cups)
      2   tsp dried mint leaves
    1/8   tsp cinnamon
          salt and pepper to taste
    1½   tbsp flour
    1/2   cup sour cream

Sauté onion in oil until transparent. Add parsley, broth and mint leaves. Bring to a boil and remove from heat. Add cinnamon and purée in blender, a portion at a time. Add salt and pepper. In soup pan mix flour with 1/4 cup sour cream. Gradually add the soup and return to heat. Bring to a boil and simmer, stirring until slightly thickened. Serve hot or cold and garnish with remaining sour cream and a dash of cinnamon. Serves 8–10.

CRABMEAT SOUP

      1   can (10½-oz) cream of tomato soup
      1   can (10½-oz) cream of mushroom soup
      1   can (10½-oz) green pea soup
      2   soup cans milk
      1   pkg (6-oz) frozen crabmeat, thawed, drained and flaked
    1/3   cup dry sherry
          Garnish: parsley

Combine undiluted soups and heat over hot water, stirring until well blended. Stir in milk and crabmeat. To serve: stir in sherry and garnish with chopped parsley. Serve hot. Serves 6–8.

EGG AND LEMON SOUP

3 cans (13¾-oz) chicken broth (5¼ cups)
3 tbsp raw rice
3 eggs
  juice of 1½ lemons
  salt to taste
  Garnish: parsley

Bring broth to boil and add rice. Cook about 15 min. or until rice is tender. To serve: beat eggs until light and fluffy. Add lemon juice. Stir about 2 cups of hot soup into egg-lemon mixture. Return this mixture to the rest of the broth, beating constantly. Heat, do not boil. Serve immediately garnished with chopped parsley. Serves 6–8.

PIMIENTO-CHEESE SOUP

5 tbsp butter
1 onion, chopped
3 pimientos, chopped
5 tbsp flour
1¼ cans (13¾-oz) chicken broth (2¼ cups)
1 envelope instant chicken broth mix
1 cup milk
1 cup light cream
1½ cups grated Cheddar cheese
3/4 tsp basil
  salt and pepper to taste
  Garnish: parsley

Melt butter and sauté onion and pimiento until onion is transparent. Blend in flour. Gradually add broth, instant broth mix, milk and cream. Heat, stirring until soup thickens. Add cheese and stir until melted. Add seasoning. Serve garnished with chopped parsley. Serves 6.

Breads

The triumph of pulling freshly baked bread from an oven is everyone's ideal of the ultimate in homemaking. As much as we sometimes wish we could return to the days and ways of early America, modern living does not allow time for the kneadings and risings of our grandmother's breads. With ten minutes to spare today's cook can put together a recipe for a "quick" bread and produce almost effortlessly a piping hot loaf of spicy pumpkin, scrumptious lemon or elegant cranberry tea breads.

The distinctive ingredient in quick breads is baking powder. Until the late eighteenth century, lightness in breads was achieved by laboriously beating air into the dough along with the eggs. By the 1850's a new and improved baking powder revolutionized the bread-baking scene. Making bread was now simple, quick and failure free. A thorough-going knowledge of the peculiarities of yeast was no longer a prerequisite to receiving the greatest compliment in cookery—"she even bakes her own bread."

The tastes and textures of nut and fruit breads are a perfect accompaniment to a light ladies' luncheon. Always select a bread to complement the entrée served—a sweet-flavored loaf with a tart salad, a rich variety with a light soup, or a crunchy, textured bread with an airy fish mousse. For added attractiveness, bake the loaves in 1 lb. cans filled three-fourths full, or make small individual loaves by using baby food juice cans. Always allow time to cool before slicing. Quick breads slice best after being wrapped in foil and refrigerated overnight.

All the bread recipes for LADIES WHO LUNCH can be frozen for as long as a month by carefully wrapping the loaves in foil and sealing in a plastic bag for freezer storage.

APPLESAUCE RAISIN BREAD

1½	cups raisins
2	cups sifted flour
3/4	cup sugar
3	tsp baking powder
2	tsp cinnamon
1	tsp salt
1/2	tsp baking soda
1	egg, beaten
1½	cups applesauce
2	tbsp butter, melted

Preheat oven to 350°.

Barely cover raisins with water and simmer for 10 min. to plump fruit. Sift together flour, sugar, baking powder, cinnamon, salt and baking soda. Combine egg, applesauce and butter and stir into flour mixture until just blended. Add plumped raisins. Pour batter into a greased 9″ x 5″ loaf pan. Bake 1 hr. or until a toothpick inserted into loaf comes out clean. To freeze: let cool and wrap securely in foil. Yield: 1 loaf.

APRICOT-NUT BREAD

      1   box (11-oz) dried apricots
    1/4   cup hot water
      1   cup sugar
      2   cups sifted flour
      2   tsp baking powder
    1/2   tsp baking soda
      1   tsp salt
      2   eggs, beaten
    1/2   cup orange juice
      2   tbsp butter, melted
    1/2   cup chopped pecans

Preheat oven to 375°.
Soak apricots in hot water for 30 min. Drain and chop them. Sift dry ingredients together and gradually stir in eggs, orange juice and butter. Add the apricots and pecans to the batter and mix thoroughly. Pour into greased 9" x 5" loaf pan and bake for about 1 hr. or until toothpick inserted into loaf comes out clean. To freeze: let cool and wrap securely in foil. Yield: 1 loaf.

MELBA TOAST VARIATIONS

     12   slices of very thin, day old bread
    1/4   cup butter, softened

Preheat oven to 350°.
Remove crusts from bread and spread lightly with butter. Place on cookie sheet and bake at 350° about 15 min. or until brown. Leave toast in 200° oven for about 1 hr. until very dry.
POPPY SEED STICKS: remove crusts and butter bread. Cut into 4 strips. Sprinkle generously with poppy seed. Bake as above.
MELBA TOAST CURLS: remove crusts and butter bread. Fold over 2 diagonally opposite corners a little past the middle and pin in position with a toothpick. Bake as above. Remove toothpick and serve. Yield: 12 Toasts or 48 Sticks.

APPLE-CHEESE-NUT BREAD

2	cups sifted flour
1	tsp baking powder
1/2	tsp baking soda
1	tsp salt
1/2	cup butter, softened
2/3	cup sugar
1/4	tsp nutmeg
2	eggs
1⅓	cup ground apple, unpeeled
1/2	cup grated sharp Cheddar cheese
1/4	cup chopped walnuts

Preheat oven to 350°.
Sift flour, baking powder, soda and salt together. Cream butter with sugar and nutmeg. Add eggs, beating until light and fluffy. Add ground apples, cheese and walnuts to the butter mixture. Add the dry ingredients, mixing only until flour disappears. Pour batter into greased 9" x 5" loaf pan. Bake 1 hr. or until toothpick inserted into loaf comes out clean. To freeze: let cool and wrap securely in foil. Yield: 1 loaf.

CRANBERRY BREAD

2	cups sifted flour
1/2	tsp salt
1½	tsp baking powder
1/2	tsp baking soda
1	cup sugar
2	eggs, beaten
2	tbsp butter, melted
2	tbsp hot water
6	tbsp orange juice
2	tbsp lemon juice
1/4	cup grated orange rind

1   cup cranberries, cut up
1/2 cup chopped pecans (optional)

Preheat oven to 325°.

Sift the dry ingredients together. Combine eggs, butter, water, orange and lemon juices and orange rind. Add to dry ingredients, mixing thoroughly. Fold in cranberries and nuts. Pour batter into greased 9" x 5" loaf pan and bake for about 1 hr. or until a toothpick inserted into the loaf comes out clean. To freeze: let cool and wrap securely in foil. Yield: 1 loaf.

LEMON BREAD

1½   cups sifted flour
1   tsp, baking powder
1/2 tsp salt
5   tbsp butter, softened
1   cup sugar
2   eggs

1/2 cup milk
     grated rind of 2 lemons
1/2 cup finely chopped pecans (optional)

     GLAZE

     juice of 1 lemon
1/2 cup sugar

Preheat oven to 350°.

Sift flour, baking powder and salt together. Cream butter with sugar. Add eggs, beating until light and fluffy. Thoroughly blend into flour mixture. Stir in milk, lemon rind and pecans. Pour batter in greased 9" x 5" loaf pan. Bake for 1 hr. or until toothpick inserted in loaf comes out clean.

GLAZE: mix lemon juice and sugar together until sugar dissolves. Spoon glaze over bread immediately after removing from oven. To freeze: let cool and wrap securely in foil. Yield: 1 loaf.

BANANA BREAD

1½   cups sifted flour
2   tsp baking powder
1/2   tsp salt
1/2   cup butter, softened
1   cup sugar
2   eggs
1   tsp vanilla
1   cup mashed banana, very ripe
1/4   cup buttermilk
    or
1/2   cup sour cream

Preheat oven to 350°.
Sift flour, baking powder and salt together. Cream butter with sugar. Add eggs and vanilla, beating until light and fluffy. Add dry ingredients alternately with banana and buttermilk or sour cream to butter mixture. Stir until well blended. Pour batter in greased 9" x 5" loaf pan. Bake for 1 hr. or until a toothpick inserted in the loaf comes out clean. To freeze: let cool and wrap securely in foil. Yield: 1 loaf.

SESAME BREAD

1/2   cup plus 1 tbsp sesame seed
1/4   cup butter, softened
2/3   cup sugar
2   eggs
3   cups sifted flour
2½   tsp baking powder
3/4   tsp salt
1½   tsp grated lemon rind
1½   cups milk

Preheat oven to 350°.
Toast 1/2 cup sesame seed in oven for 15–20 min. until brown.
Cream butter with sugar and add eggs, beating until light and
fluffy. Sift flour, baking powder and salt together and add toasted
sesame seed. Add dry ingredients to egg mixture alternately with
lemon rind and milk. Stir until just blended. Pour batter into
greased 9" x 5" loaf pan. Sprinkle 1 tbsp. sesame seed on top.
Bake for 1 hr. and 10 min. or until toothpick inserted in loaf comes
out clean. To serve: slice very thin and spread with sweet butter
or cream cheese. To freeze: let cool and wrap securely in foil.
Yield: 1 loaf.

COCONUT BREAD

2	cups sifted flour
2	tsp baking powder
1/2	tsp salt
1/2	cup butter, softened
3/4	cup sugar
2	eggs
1	banana, mashed
1	can (3½-oz) shredded coconut
2	tbsp grated orange peel
1/4	cup cold milk
1/2	cup chopped walnuts or pecans (optional)

Preheat oven to 350°.
Sift flour, baking powder and salt together. Cream butter with
sugar. Add eggs, beating until light and fluffy. Add the banana,
coconut, orange peel and milk, blending thoroughly. Gradually
stir in dry ingredients. Pour batter into greased 9" x 5" loaf pan.
Bake for 1 hr. and 15 min. or until a toothpick inserted into the
loaf comes out clean. Loaf is best when stored a day before slicing.
To freeze: let cool and wrap securely in foil. Yield: 1 loaf.

NUT BREAD

        1   cup sifted flour
        2   tsp baking powder
        1   tsp salt
        1   cup whole wheat flour
        1   tsp butter, softened
      2/3   cup sugar
        1   egg, beaten
        1   cup buttermilk
      1/2   cup finely chopped pecans
      1/4   cup blanched, finely chopped almonds
      1/4   cup finely chopped walnuts

Preheat oven to 350°.
Sift flour, baking powder and salt together and gently stir in whole
wheat flour. Cream butter with sugar. Add egg, beating until light
and fluffy. Stir in flour mixture alternately with buttermilk. Beat
until batter is smooth. Fold in nut meats and pour into greased
9" x 5" loaf pan. Let stand for 30 min. Bake for 1 hr. or until
toothpick inserted into loaf comes out clean. To freeze: let cool
and wrap securely in foil. Yield: 1 loaf.

ITALIAN CRESCENTS

        1   pkg (8-oz) refrigerated crescent rolls
      1/4   cup commercial barbeque sauce
      1/8   tsp oregano
      1/8   tsp basil
      1/8   tsp thyme
        3   ounces of Swiss cheese, sliced

Preheat oven to 375°.
Unroll crescents and separate into 8 triangles. Mix barbeque
sauce and seasoning and brush each triangle with a small amount
of sauce. Make 16 strips of cheese (1/2" x 2") and place 2 cheese
strips on each triangle. Roll and bake according to package directions. Yield: 8 rolls.

CARAWAY BREAD

2 cups sifted flour
1½ tsp baking powder
1/4 tsp salt
2 tbsp caraway seed
1/2 cup butter, softened
1 cup sugar
2 eggs
1/2 cup milk

Preheat oven to 350°.
Sift flour, baking powder and salt together. Add caraway seed.
Cream butter with sugar. Add eggs, beating until light and fluffy.
Stir in flour mixture alternately with the milk until well blended.
Pour batter into greased 9" x 5" loaf pan and bake for about 1 hr.
or until a toothpick inserted into loaf comes out clean. To freeze:
let cool and wrap securely in foil. Yield: 1 loaf.

SPICE BREAD

1⅓ cups sifted flour
1½ tsp cinnamon
1½ tsp baking soda
1/2 tsp salt
1⅓ cups sugar
3 eggs, beaten
2 cups minced carrots
2/3 cup salad oil
1/2 cup chopped walnuts

Preheat oven to 375°.
Sift dry ingredients together. Combine eggs, carrots and oil and
thoroughly blend into flour mixture. Stir in nuts. Pour batter into
9" x 5" greased loaf pan and bake for 1 hr. or until a toothpick
inserted into the loaf comes out clean. To freeze: let cool and
wrap securely in foil. Yield: 1 loaf.

BREADS 27

BLUEBERRY BREAD

3 cups sifted flour plus 2 tbsp
1 tsp salt
4 tsp baking powder
2 eggs, beaten
1 cup sugar
1 cup milk
1/4 cup butter, melted
2 cups fresh blueberries
1 tsp cinnamon

Preheat oven to 350°.
Sift 3 cups flour, salt and baking powder together. Combine eggs and sugar and stir in milk and butter. Add to flour mixture and stir until just combined, not smooth. Toss blueberries with the 2 tbsp. of flour and the cinnamon. Add to batter, stirring only a few times. Pour batter into a greased 9" x 5" loaf pan. Bake for 45–50 min. or until a toothpick inserted into the loaf comes out clean. To freeze: let cool and wrap securely in foil. Yield: 1 loaf.

BUTTER PECAN CIRCLES

2 cups sifted flour
2 tsp baking powder
1/2 tsp baking soda
1/2 tsp salt
1 tsp cinnamon
1/4 tsp nutmeg
1 cup light brown sugar, packed
1 egg, beaten
1 cup buttermilk

2 tbsp butter, melted
1 cup broken pecans

Preheat oven to 350°.
Sift together flour, baking powder, baking soda, salt, cinnamon and nutmeg. Blend in brown sugar. Combine egg, buttermilk and butter and thoroughly stir into flour mixture. Mix in nuts. Pour batter into a greased 9" x 5" loaf pan. Bake for 45–50 min. or until a toothpick inserted into loaf comes out clean. For an interesting shape, bake in 2 greased 1-lb. size cans, filled about two-thirds full. To freeze: let cool and wrap securely in foil. Yield: 1 loaf.

PINEAPPLE AND WALNUT BREAD

  2   cups sifted flour
  3   tsp baking powder
  1   tsp salt
1/2   tsp baking soda
1/4   cup butter, softened
1/2   cup sugar
1½   tsp vanilla
  1   egg
1/3   cup finely chopped dates
3/4   cup finely chopped walnuts
  1   can (1-lb 4½-oz) crushed pineapple, drained

Preheat oven to 350°.
Sift flour, baking powder, salt and baking soda together. Cream butter with sugar and vanilla. Add egg, beating until light and fluffy. Add dry ingredients. Stir in dates, walnuts and *drained* pineapple. Pour into greased 9" x 5" loaf pan. Bake 1 hr. or until a toothpick inserted into loaf comes out clean. To freeze: let cool and wrap securely in foil. Yield: 1 loaf.

MARMALADE BREAD

2 cups sifted flour
3 tsp baking powder
1 tsp salt
1 jar (1-lb) orange marmalade
1 egg, beaten
1/2 cup orange juice
1/4 cup butter, melted
1 cup chopped walnuts (optional)

Preheat oven to 350°.
Sift flour with baking powder and salt. Reserve 1/4 cup of marmalade. Combine 1¼ cup marmalade, egg, orange juice and butter. Add to flour mixture, stirring until thoroughly blended. Fold in nuts. Pour batter into greased 9" x 5" loaf pan. Bake for about 1 hr. or until a toothpick inserted into the loaf comes out clean. Remove from pan, spread top with reserved marmalade and return to oven for about 1 min. or until top is glazed. To freeze: let cool and wrap securely in foil. Yield 1 loaf.

HERB STICKS

4 tbsp butter
1/4 tsp basil
1/4 tsp oregano
1/4 tsp thyme
1/4 tsp garlic powder
10 slices thinly sliced bread

Preheat oven to 200°.
Combine butter and herbs in a small saucepan and simmer for 20 min. Remove crusts from bread and spread with herb-butter mixture. Cut each slice of bread in thirds. Bake for about 30 min. for crisp bread sticks or 10 min. for soft bread sticks. This herb-butter mixture may also be spread between slices of French or Italian loaves. Wrap the loaf in foil and bake at 350° for about 20 min. Yield: 30 bread sticks or 1 small loaf.

MUFFINS

    2   cups sifted flour
    2   tbsp sugar
   2½   tsp baking powder
   1/2   tsp salt
    1   egg, beaten
    1   cup milk
   1/4   cup butter, melted

Preheat oven to 400°.
Sift together dry ingredients. Combine egg, milk and butter and
add to dry ingredients, mixing by hand only until flour disappears,
or about 10 strokes. Pour batter into greased muffin tins, filling
about half full. Bake for 20 min. Yield: 20 muffins.
BLUEBERRY MUFFINS: increase sugar to 1/4 cup and add 3/4 cup
blueberries to dry ingredients.
DATE-NUT MUFFINS: add 1/2 cup chopped nuts and 1/2 cup
chopped pitted dates to dry ingredients.
BANANA MUFFINS: add 3/4 cup mashed banana to dry ingredients.
BACON MUFFINS: substitute 2 tbsp. bacon fat for 2 tbsp. of butter.
Add 6–8 slices cooked, crumbled bacon to dry ingredients.

PARMESAN CHEESE WAFERS

   1/2   lb butter, softened
    1   cup freshly grated Parmesan cheese
    2   cups sifted flour
    1   tsp baking powder
    1   tsp salt

Cream butter and cheese together until well blended. Sift together
flour, baking powder and salt. Blend into cheese mixture. Shape
dough into a roll about 1½" diameter for slicing and baking. Chill
until dough can be easily sliced. Slices should be about 1/2" thick.
Bake in 400° oven for 10–12 min. Serve hot. To freeze: wrap roll
securely in foil. Yield: about 36 wafers.

BREADS   31

CHEESE AND BACON SPOON BREAD

        3/4   cup cornmeal
        1½   cups water
        2   cups grated Cheddar cheese
        1/4   cup butter, softened
        1   tsp garlic powder
        1/2   tsp salt
        1   cup milk
        4   egg yolks, beaten
        6   slices crisply cooked bacon
        4   egg whites, beaten stiff

Preheat oven to 325°.
Combine cornmeal and water. Cook, stirring constantly until thickened. Remove from heat. Add cheese, butter, garlic powder and salt, stirring until cheese melts. Add milk and egg yolks. Crumble bacon and thoroughly mix into batter. Just before baking, fold in egg whites. Pour batter into a greased 2-qt. casserole. Bake for about 1 hr. or until brown and puffy. To serve: garnish with a dab of butter and serve with spoons. Serves 6.

BETH'S PUMPKIN BREAD

        3½   cups sifted flour
        2   tsp baking soda
        1½   tsp salt
        2   tsp cinnamon
        2   tsp nutmeg
        1   tsp pumpkin spice
        3   cups sugar
        1   cup salad oil
        4   eggs
        2/3   cup water
        1   can (1-lb) pumpkin

Preheat oven to 350°.
Sift dry ingredients together in a large bowl. The spices should be

measured as heaping teaspoons. Make a well in the center of the bowl and add the remaining ingredients. Mix thoroughly until smooth. Grease either one 9" x 5" loaf pan or two 7" x 3" loaf pans. Pour in batter and bake for 1 hr. or until a toothpick inserted into the loaf comes out clean. To freeze: let cool and wrap securely in foil. Yield: 1 large or 2 small loaves.

CORN BREAD

1/2	cup sifted flour
1/2	cup cornmeal
	salt to taste
4	tsp baking powder
5	tbsp butter, melted
1	cup sugar
4	eggs, beaten
1/3	cup milk

Preheat oven to 375°.
Sift flour with cornmeal, salt and baking powder. Cream butter with sugar. Add eggs, beating until light and fluffy. Add dry ingredients and stir in milk. Pour into greased 8" x 12" shallow baking dish and bake for about 25 min. or until a toothpick inserted in bread comes out clean. To freeze: let cool and wrap securely in foil. Serves 8–10.

NEVER-FALL POPOVERS

1	cup sifted flour
1/2	tsp salt
2	eggs, beaten
1	cup cold milk

Combine flour and salt and sift over beaten eggs. Add milk all at once and beat until smooth. Fill greased popover pans two-thirds full and put in cold oven. Set oven at 450° and bake for 30 min. or until brown. Yield: 8 popovers.

PINWHEEL ONION ROLLS

      1/4   cup plus 2 tbsp butter
        4   medium onions, thinly sliced
        2   tsp salt
        2   cups sifted flour
        3   tsp baking powder
      2/3   cup milk
        1   egg
        1   tbsp cream

Preheat oven to 400°.
Melt 2 tbsp. butter and sauté onions with 1 tsp. of salt until onions
are transparent. Cool. Sift flour, baking powder and remaining 1
tsp. of salt together. Cut in 1/4 cup butter with pastry blender or
fingers until the consistency of coarse cornmeal. Add milk and mix
with a fork until dough forms a ball. Roll out on floured board into
a 12" square. Spread with onions. Roll up as for a jelly roll. Chill
for at least 2 hr. Cut into twelve 1" slices. Place flat side down on
a cookie sheet. Beat egg with cream and brush slices. Bake for
about 20 min. Serve immediately with sweet butter. To freeze:
wrap unbaked roll of dough securely in foil. Defrost only enough
to slice and bake as above. Yield: 12 rolls.

SCONES

        2   cups sifted flour
        2   tbsp sugar
        1   tbsp baking powder
      1/2   tsp salt
      1/2   cup butter
      1/2   cup raisins
        1   egg, beaten
      1/2   cup light cream

Preheat oven to 425°.

Sift dry ingredients together. Cut butter into flour mixture until it is the consistency of coarse meal. Stir in raisins. Make a well in center of mixture and add egg which has been combined with the cream. Stir with a fork until dough forms a ball. Knead lightly on a floured surface 10–15 times. Roll dough into a circle 1/2″ thick. Cut into 12 wedges. Place wedges on greased baking sheet. Bake for about 15 min. To serve: split wedges and spread with butter. Yield: 12 scones.

SESAME SEED STICKS

1/4	cup plus 2 tbsp butter
1/2	cup sesame seed
1	cup plus 2 tbsp sifted flour
2	tsp sugar
2	tsp baking powder
3/4	tsp salt
1/2	cup milk
1	egg white

Preheat oven to 450°.
Melt 2 tbsp. butter and combine with 1/4 cup of sesame seed. Spread seed in baking pan and bake for 5–8 min. until brown. Sift dry ingredients together. Add milk and mix well. Turn out on a lightly floured board. Add toasted sesame seed and knead about 10 times. Roll out dough into a 10″ x 7″ rectangle. Cut in 1/2″ x 4″ strips. Meanwhile, melt remaining 1/4 cup butter. Coat the strips in butter and lay in rows in 8″ x 12″ baking dish. Brush tops with egg white. Sprinkle with remaining 1/4 cup sesame seed. Bake for 5–8 min. Do not overbake. Serve immediately. Yield: 24 sticks.

ORANGE BISCUITS

2 cups sifted flour
2 tbsp sugar
2½ tsp double-acting baking powder
1/4 tsp salt
1 tbsp grated orange rind
5 tbsp butter
2/3 cup light cream
1 tbsp orange marmalade

Preheat oven to 425°.
Sift flour, sugar, baking powder and salt together in a bowl. Add orange rind. Cut butter into flour mixture with two knives or a pastry blender until it is the consistency of coarse meal. Stir in cream to form a soft dough. Turn dough out on lightly floured board and knead about 10 times. Roll out dough 3/4" thick and cut rounds with a 1½" biscuit cutter. Make an indentation in the center of each round and fill it with 1/4 tsp. of orange marmalade. Place on greased cookie sheet. Bake for 12–15 min. or until puffed and golden. Yield: 12 biscuits.

SOUR CREAM AND CHIVE BISCUITS

2 cups sifted flour
2½ tsp double-acting baking powder
1 tsp salt
3/4 cup sour cream
1/2 cup chopped chives
1/2–2/3 cup milk

Preheat oven to 425°.
Sift flour, baking powder and salt together in a bowl. Add sour cream and chives. Stir in milk to form a soft dough. Turn dough out on a lightly floured board and knead about 10 times. Roll dough 3/4" thick and cut rounds with a 1½" biscuit cutter. Place on greased cookie sheet. Bake for 12–15 min. until puffed and golden. Yield: 12 biscuits.

CHEDDAR CHEESE WAFERS

          1/2   lb butter, softened
            1   cup grated sharp Cheddar cheese
        1½   cups sifted flour
            1   tsp salt
                 dash of cayenne pepper
          1/2   tsp garlic powder
            1   tsp thyme

Cream butter and cheese together until well blended. Add remaining ingredients. Shape dough into a roll about 1½" diameter for slicing and baking. Chill until dough can be easily sliced. Slices should be about 1/2" thick. Bake in 400° oven for 10–12 min. Serve hot or cold. To freeze: wrap roll securely in foil. Yield: about 36 wafers.

BLUE CHEESE BISCUITS

            2   cups sifted flour
            4   tsp double-acting baking powder
            1   tsp salt
          1/4   cup plus 2 tbsp butter
          1/2   cup blue cheese
      1/2–2/3   cup plus 1 tbsp milk

Preheat oven to 425°.
Sift flour, baking powder and salt together in a bowl. Cut 1/4 cup butter and cheese into the flour mixture until it is the consistency of coarse meal. Stir in 1/2–2/3 cup milk to form a soft dough. Turn dough out on a lightly floured board and knead about 10 times. Roll dough 3/4" thick and cut rounds with a 1½" biscuit cutter. Melt remaining 2 tbsp. butter, add 1 tbsp. milk and brush rounds. Place on greased cookie sheet and bake for 10–12 min. or until puffed and golden. Yield 12 biscuits.

CHEESE POPOVERS
Blender

    1   cup milk
    1   cup grated Cheddar cheese
    2   eggs
    1   cup sifted flour
  1/4   tsp salt

Preheat oven to 425°.
Place all ingredients in blender and blend for 20 sec. Pour batter into heated, greased popover pans or muffin pans, filling the pans two-thirds full. Bake for about 45 min. or until puffy and brown. Serve immediately. Yield: 8–10 popovers.

Entrées

A luncheon invitation is a special treat. It is a change from every day's hectic activities and the usual baloney sandwich or can of soup. Ladies look forward to enjoying the cook's best. With the coming of entire cooking courses on the home television screen, not to mention the innumerable cookbooks on every kitchen shelf, there is a great deal more expected at a luncheon than chicken à la king and a store-bought petits fours. These entrées for LADIES WHO LUNCH will treat your guests to different tastes and flavors and even some exotic international dishes. Best of all, the recipes are simple to prepare and do not require hours of marinating or simmering.

It is not necessary to have a large collection of cooking and serving equipment on hand. However, every cook should indulge herself in a few special culinary tools. A fish mousse looks and tastes better served from a fish mold and garnished appropriately. There are all kinds of molds in different shapes and sizes for gelatin recipes. Soufflé dishes, individual ramekins and scallop shells for seafood add to the attractiveness of the table. Use a quiche pan and produce a French cooking school effect rather than a plain-looking custard pie. Freezer-to-oven-to-table casseroles are helpful when preparing the food in advance.

The entrée is the mainstay of the menu and should be chosen with care to fit the occasion and the season. If it is a formal luncheon using the best linen and silver, serve elegant crêpes or a quiche. For an informal get-together, a puffy ham and Swiss cheese sandwich is just the thing. There are chilled soups and salads for summer and hearty casseroles and hot soups for winter. A thought to remember—a ladies' luncheon is not dinner. The entrée should be served in such a manner as to make an eye-catching entrance from the kitchen and be enough just to barely satisfy the taste. Dessert is yet to come.

SOUR CREAM SOUFFLÉ

1½	cups sour cream
3/4	cup sifted flour
1¼	tsp salt
1/4	tsp pepper
2	tbsp chopped chives
1/2	cup grated nonprocessed Gruyere cheese
5	eggs, separated

Preheat oven to 350°.
Thoroughly blend sour cream, flour, salt and pepper. Stir in chives and grated cheese. Beat egg yolks until thick and stir into the cheese mixture. Beat egg whites until stiff and carefully fold into the mixture. Pour into a 2-qt. soufflé dish. Place dish in shallow pan of hot water and bake about 30–40 min. or until puffed and set. Serve immediately. Serves 6.

WELSH RAREBIT

    1/2   lb sharp Cheddar cheese, crumbled
      1   jar (8-oz) commercial processed cheese spread
    3/4   cup heavy cream
    1/2   tsp dry mustard
    1/4   tsp salt
    1/2   tsp Worcestershire sauce
          dash of pepper
      1   tbsp dry sherry
          toast points

Melt cheese over hot water. Gradually stir in the remaining ingredients. Serve on toast points.
Beer or gingerale may be used in place of the cream. Omit the sherry.
Turkey or chicken slices may be placed on the toast and the hot rarebit poured over the meat. Place on a broil proof platter. Heat under broiler until bubbly. Serves 6.

TOMATO WELSH RAREBIT

      1/4   lb butter
        4   tbsp flour
        1   can (10½-oz) tomato soup
        1   lb grated sharp Cheddar cheese
      1/2   tsp salt
              white pepper to taste
        1   medium onion, grated
  1/2–3/4   cup milk or light cream
              toast points
              Garnish: crisp bacon

Melt butter and stir in flour until well blended. Gradually add tomato soup, cheese, salt, pepper and onion, stirring constantly. Cook, stirring, until sauce is thickened and smooth. Add milk or cream gradually until desired consistency is obtained. Serve on toast points with strips of crisp bacon. Serves 6–8.

CHEESE SOUFFLÉ

6 tbsp butter
6 tbsp flour
1½ cups milk
1/3 tsp salt
1/8 tsp pepper
1/3 tsp dry mustard
dash of cayenne pepper
1½ cups shredded sharp Cheddar cheese
5 eggs, separated
1/4 tsp cream of tartar

Preheat oven to 350°.
Melt butter and stir in flour until well blended. Gradually add milk and seasonings, stirring constantly. Cook, stirring, over low heat until sauce is thickened and smooth. Mix the cheese into the hot sauce. Remove from heat and stir in 5 beaten egg yolks. Beat egg whites with cream of tartar until stiff. Fold the cheese mixture into the egg whites. Pour into a buttered 2-qt. soufflé dish. Set dish in pan of warm water. Bake for 45–50 min. or until puffed and golden brown. Serve soufflé immediately. Serves 6.

CHEESE AND MUSHROOM PUFFS

1 tbsp butter
1/2 cup finely chopped mushrooms
2 tsp grated onion
2 eggs, separated
1/2 lb grated Swiss cheese
1/2 tsp salt
1/8 tsp pepper
1 tsp Worcestershire sauce
6 slices of bread, crusts removed, toasted on one side

Preheat oven to 375°.

Melt butter and sauté mushrooms and onion until onions are transparent. Beat egg yolks and combine with cheese, salt, pepper and Worcestershire sauce. Stir into mushroom mixture. Beat egg whites until stiff and fold into cheese and mushroom mixture. Lightly butter untoasted side of bread and place on baking sheet, buttered side up. Spoon mixture on top. Bake until puffy and brown. Serve immediately. Serves 6.

EGGS IN CHEESE BASKET

PASTRY

1	cup sifted flour
1/4	tsp salt
1/3	cup butter
1/4	cup grated Cheddar cheese
3–5	tbsp cold water

FILLING

1	can (4½-oz) deviled ham
6	eggs
	salt and pepper to taste
	Cheese Sauce (p. 95)

Preheat oven to 450°.

PASTRY: mix the flour and salt. Cut in butter and cheese with pastry blender or fingers until the consistency of coarse meal. Sprinkle water, 1 tbsp. at a time, over the mixture and stir with a fork until it can be gathered into a ball. Do not overwork dough. On a floured board roll out dough into a rectangle about 1/8" thick. Lightly grease 6 muffin tins. Cut 6 squares of pastry large enough to fit into tins so that dough extends over edges for sealing. FILLING: divide deviled ham into each pastry lined tin. Break an egg into each cup. Season with salt and pepper. Pull corners of pastry together as if to form a basket and seal. Bake for about 20 min. or until brown. Serve with Cheese Sauce. Serves 6.

ENTRÉES   43

DEVILED EGGS AND SHRIMP IN MORNAY SAUCE

           6 hard-boiled eggs
        1/4 tsp dry mustard
        1/3 cup chopped parsley
        1/2 cup mayonnaise
        1½ lbs small cooked shrimp
        3/4 cup freshly grated Parmesan cheese

           MORNAY SAUCE

           3 tbsp butter
           3 tbsp flour
        3/4 cup chicken broth
        3/4 cup light or heavy cream
           4 ounces Gruyere cheese, grated
           1 tbsp dry sherry

Preheat oven to 350°.
Cut eggs in half lengthwise and put yolks in a bowl. Thoroughly
mash yolks and mix in mustard, parsley and about 1/2 cup
mayonnaise or enough to make a smooth paste. Fill each egg
white half with the yolk mixture. Place in buttered ovenproof
serving dish and distribute shrimp evenly around the eggs. Prepare
the sauce.

MORNAY SAUCE: melt butter and stir in flour until well blended.
Gradually add chicken broth and cream, stirring constantly. Cook,
stirring over low heat until sauce is thickened and smooth. Add
the Gruyere cheese and heat, stirring until cheese melts. Add
sherry.
Spoon sauce over egg and shrimp. Sprinkle with Parmesan cheese
and heat for 15 min. to warm thoroughly. Remove from oven and
place under broiler for 3–4 min. or until top is golden brown.
Serves 6.

EGGS MORNAY

6	tbsp butter
2	tbsp minced onion
1/2	cup sliced mushrooms
6	tbsp flour
1¾	cups milk
1	cup chicken broth
1	envelope instant chicken broth mix
3/4	cup grated Cheddar cheese
1/2	cup freshly grated Parmesan cheese
1/4	cup dry sherry
1	tsp Worcestershire sauce
	salt and pepper to taste
12	hard-boiled eggs, sliced
	croutons
1	tbsp butter

Melt butter and sauté onions and mushrooms until onions are transparent. Stir in flour and blend well. Gradually add milk, chicken broth and instant broth mix. Cook, stirring over low heat until sauce is thickened and smooth. Stir in cheeses, sherry and Worcestershire sauce. Add salt and pepper. Fold in egg slices. Spoon into 6 individual ramekins. Top each with croutons and 1/2 tsp. butter. Sprinkle with additional Parmesan cheese and brown under broiler. Serves 6.

EGGS BENEDICT

2	tbsp butter
12	thin slices of baked or boiled ham
6	English muffins, halved and toasted on one side
12	poached eggs
1½	cups Hollandaise Sauce (p. 98)

Melt butter and sauté ham for about 1 min. on each side. Place hot ham on muffin. Top with hot poached egg and cover with warm Hollandaise Sauce. There are 2 eggs per serving. Serves 6.

CURRIED EGGS

1/3	cup butter
1	onion, chopped
1/2	tsp garlic powder
1	tbsp flour
2	tbsp curry powder
1½	tbsp ketchup
1	cup beef or chicken broth
	salt to taste
	lemon juice to taste
9	hard-boiled eggs
3	cups cooked rice
	Condiments: chopped peanuts, chutney, coconut, chopped green onion

Melt butter and sauté onion and garlic powder until onion is transparent. Stir in flour, curry powder and ketchup until well blended. Gradually add broth. Cook, stirring until sauce is slightly thickened and smooth. Season with salt and lemon juice. Simmer for 10 min. Carefully cut eggs lengthwise in quarters and fold into sauce. Serve on rice with side dishes of condiments for guests to choose their own. Serves 6.

EGGS FLORENTINE

1/4	cup butter
1/4	cup flour
1	cup milk
1	cup light cream
1/2	tsp salt
	freshly ground black pepper to taste
1/2	tsp nutmeg
2	pkg (10-oz) chopped spinach, cooked and drained
12	poached eggs
	freshly grated Parmesan cheese

46   *ENTRÉES*

Melt butter and stir in flour until smooth. Gradually add milk, cream, salt, pepper, and nutmeg, stirring constantly until sauce is thickened and smooth. Combine hot spinach with 1/2 cup of the sauce. Spread spinach mixture in a 11" x 16" baking dish and arrange eggs on top. Pour remaining hot sauce over eggs and sprinkle liberally with Parmesan cheese. Broil 3–5 min. until sauce is bubbly and top is brown. There are 2 eggs per serving. Note: this dish may be prepared ahead of time and assembled at the last minute. Poach eggs early in the day until just set. Plunge them immediately into ice water. Refrigerate in ice water until serving time. Just before serving, cook spinach, reheat sauce, drain eggs and assemble. Cook as above. Serves 6.

EGGS IN TOMATO SHELL

6	large tomatoes
6	eggs
	salt and pepper to taste
1	tbsp basil
1	tbsp oregano
2	tbsp butter
6	tbsp freshly grated Parmesan cheese
	Garnish: parsley or water cress

Preheat oven to 350°.
Peel tomatoes and scoop out a hole in center, large enough to contain an egg. Break raw egg into tomato shells. Season each with salt and pepper, 1/2 tsp. basil and orègano and 1 tsp. butter. Top each with 1 tbsp. Parmesan cheese. Bake for about 25–30 min. or until eggs are just set. Garnish with parsley or water cress. Serves 6.

BASIC LUNCHEON CRÊPES

        2/3   cup flour
        1/2   tsp salt
          3   eggs
          1   cup milk (or 1/2 milk and 1/2 chicken broth)
          3   tbsp butter, melted

Combine flour and salt. Lightly beat eggs and sift flour mixture over top and beat until smooth. Stir in milk and melted butter. Let stand for an hour. Lightly grease a 6" skillet and heat. When a drop of water sizzles and rolls off skillet, it is ready for use. Spoon 3 tbsp (approximately 1½ ounces) of batter into pan and rotate quickly so that batter covers bottom. Cook crêpes quickly, until golden on both sides. Be sure to lightly grease pan before preparing each crêpe. Crêpes may be kept warm in the oven while filling is prepared, or they may be refrigerated for several days. Reheat before filling. Yield: 18 crêpes.

CRÊPES WITH CRABMEAT FILLING

          3   tbsp butter
          3   tbsp flour
        1½   cups milk
               salt and pepper to taste
        1½   cups crabmeat
        1/4   cup dry sherry
        1/4   tsp grated lemon rind
        1/4   tsp nutmeg
          1   tsp curry powder
          2   tbsp minced parsley
        3/4   cup Hollandaise Sauce (p. 98)
        1/2   cup sour cream
        1/4   cup toasted slivered almonds
         12   crêpes (p. 48)

Preheat oven to 400°.
Melt butter and stir in flour until well blended. Gradually add milk, stirring until sauce is thickened and smooth. Add salt and pepper. Stir in crabmeat, sherry, lemon rind, nutmeg, curry and parsley. Place a small amount of the crabmeat filling on each crêpe and roll as a jelly roll. Place crêpes in a buttered, shallow casserole, seam side down. Blend the Hollandaise Sauce and sour cream together and spread over top of crêpes. Sprinkle with toasted almonds and bake for 10–15 min. or until top is bubbly and golden. Serves 6.

CRÊPES WITH SALMON FILLING

1/4	cup butter
1/4	cup flour
1	tsp tarragon
1/2	tsp salt
	freshly ground pepper to taste
2	cups light cream
2	egg yolks, slightly beaten
1	can (1 lb) salmon, drained, boned and flaked
2	tbsp chopped chives
2½	tbsp white wine
1/4	cup freshly grated Parmesan cheese
12	crêpes (p. 48)

Preheat oven to 400°.
Melt butter and stir in flour until well blended. Add tarragon, salt and pepper. Gradually add cream, stirring constantly. Cook, stirring, until sauce is thickened and smooth. Stir half the hot sauce into the egg yolks. Pour back into saucepan and cook for 1 min. Blend 3/4 cup of sauce into a mixture of the salmon and chives. Place a small amount of salmon mixture on each crêpe and roll. Place crêpes in a buttered, shallow casserole, seam side down. Add wine to remaining sauce and pour over crêpes. Top with Parmesan cheese and bake for about 10 min. or until bubbly. Serves 6.

CRÊPES WITH HAM AND MUSHROOM FILLING

1/4   cup butter
1/4   cup flour
1   can (13¾ oz) chicken broth (1¾ cups)
1   cup light cream
1   tsp Worcestershire sauce
1½   tsp dry mustard
  salt and pepper to taste
1   cup cooked ham, ground
1/4   lb mushrooms, sliced
3   tbsp brandy
12   crêpes (p. 48)
2   tbsp chopped parsley
1/4   cup grated sharp Cheddar cheese

Preheat oven to 400°.
Melt butter and stir in flour until well blended. Gradually add broth and milk, stirring constantly. Cook, stirring until sauce is thickened and smooth. Add Worcestershire, mustard, salt and pepper. Blend 3/4 cup of the hot sauce into a mixture of ham and mushrooms. Place a small amount of ham mixture on each crêpe and roll as a jelly roll. Place crêpes in a buttered, shallow casserole, seam side down. Add brandy to remaining sauce and pour over crêpes. Top with parsley and grated cheese. Bake for about 10 min. or until bubbly. Serves 6.

MUSHROOM ROLL

6   eggs, separated
1½   lbs fresh mushrooms, finely chopped
1/2   cup plus 2 tbsp. butter
1½   tbsp chopped onion
3/4   tsp salt
  freshly ground pepper to taste
2   tbsp lemon juice
4–5   whole mushrooms

1½   cups Hollandaise Sauce (p. 98)
     Garnish: parsley

Preheat oven to 350°.
Beat egg yolks until fluffy. Add mushrooms. Melt 1/2 cup butter and sauté onion until transparent. Add to mushroom mixture. Stir in salt, pepper and lemon juice. Beat egg whites until stiff. Fold in mushroom mixture. Pour into a 10½" x 15½" jelly-roll pan which has been oiled and lined with oiled wax paper. Bake for 20 min. Cool and carefully turn out on to a sheet of wax paper. Peel off top paper. Gently roll up jelly-roll fashion. Cover Mushroom Roll with tinfoil and keep warm or reheat in a 250° oven. Melt remaining butter and sauté whole mushrooms over high heat until brown. Pour hot Hollandaise Sauce over roll and garnish with whole mushrooms and chopped parsley. Serves 6–8.

MUSHROOM PIE

1/2   cup butter
2   lb mushrooms, sliced
2   large onions, chopped
1/2   cup flour
     salt and pepper to taste
1   can (13¾-oz) chicken broth (1¾ cups)
2   cups light cream
1/4   cup dry sherry
1   tsp basil
     pastry for two 9" pies

Preheat oven to 375°.
Melt butter and sauté mushrooms and onions until onions are transparent. Stir in flour, salt and pepper. Gradually add chicken broth, cream and sherry, stirring constantly. Cook, stirring over low heat until sauce is thickened and smooth. Add basil and keep warm. Prepare pastry and cut to appropriate size to cover individual ramekins. Spoon warm mushroom mixture into 6–8 ramekins. Cover with pastry, seal and prick. Place immediately in oven and bake for about 15 min. or until crust is brown. Serves 6–8.

QUICHE LORRAINE

PASTRY

1 ¼	cups sifted flour
1/2	tsp salt
1	tsp sugar
2	tbsp butter
1/3	cup shortening
3	tbsp ice water
1	egg white

Preheat oven to 450°.

Sift flour with salt and sugar into a bowl. Cut in butter and shortening with pastry blender or fingers until the consistency of coarse meal. Sprinkle water over the flour mixture, mixing quickly with a fork after each addition until mixture can be gathered into a ball. Do not overwork dough. Roll out dough and line a quiche pan or a 9" pie plate, leaving a high edge. Prick bottom and sides with a fork, brush with egg white and bake for about 7 min. or until set, but not brown.

CHEESE FILLING

6	bacon slices, crisply cooked and crumbled
1	tbsp butter
1	cup cubed Swiss or Gruyere cheese
1/3	cup freshly grated Parmesan cheese
1	large onion, thinly sliced

Combine bacon, butter, cheeses and onion and sprinkle over the inside of the partly baked pastry.

CUSTARD

4	eggs, lightly beaten
3/4	cup heavy cream
3/4	cup milk
1/8	tsp salt
1/8	tsp nutmeg

Thoroughly combine all ingredients and pour custard over onion-cheese mixture in shell. Reduce oven temperature to 350° and bake for 40–45 min. until set or a knife inserted in the custard comes out clean. Cut into wedges and serve warm. Serves 6–8.

CRAB QUICHE FILLING: combine 1½ cups flaked crabmeat with 1½ cups grated Swiss cheese and 1/4 cup sliced pimiento-stuffed olives and sprinkle in baked pie shell. Pour custard over filling and bake as above.

LOBSTER QUICHE FILLING: combine 1 cup cooked cubed lobster meat, with 2 tsp. chopped celery, 1½ tbsp. chopped onion, 1½ tbsp. chopped parsley, 2 tbsp. dry sherry and 1/2 tsp. tarragon and sprinkle in baked pie shell. Pour custard over filling and bake as above.

BREAD QUICHE

1	loaf of French bread
1/2	cup butter
6	eggs, beaten
6	slices bacon, crisply fried and crumbled
1½	cups grated Swiss cheese

Preheat oven to 400°.
Cut 12–14 slices of French bread about 1/2" thick. Melt butter and lightly sauté bread. Do not brown. Place the bread in a single layer in a buttered 8" x 12" baking dish. Combine the eggs, crumbled bacon and Swiss cheese and pour over the bread. Bake for 10–15 min. or until bubbly and top is golden. Serve very hot. Serves 6–8.

TOMATO QUICHE

CRUST

1 10" baked pie shell

TOMATO PURÉE

2   tbsp butter
2/3 cup minced onion
4   large tomatoes, peeled and chopped
1/2 tsp salt
1/4 tsp pepper
1/2 tsp thyme
1   tsp parsley
1   bay leaf

Preheat oven to 350°.
Melt butter and sauté onion until transparent. Add tomatoes and seasonings and simmer, covered, for 10 min. Remove cover and increase heat. Boil until liquid has evaporated and mixture is reduced to a thick, dry purée. Remove bay leaf.

CUSTARD

4   eggs, beaten
3/4 cup heavy cream
3/4 cup milk
1/8 tsp salt
1/8 tsp nutmeg
     fresh tomato purée (recipe above)
1/4 cup freshly grated Parmesan cheese
1/4 cup grated Swiss cheese

Thoroughly combine the ingredients and pour into prepared pie shell.

TOPPING

6   1/2" slices of tomato
     salt and pepper to taste
1/2 tsp thyme

2 tbsp freshly grated Parmesan cheese
2 tbsp grated Swiss cheese
2 tbsp butter

Arrange tomato slices on custard. Top with remaining ingredients in order given. Bake for 40–45 min. until custard is set or a knife inserted in the custard comes out clean. Cut into wedges and serve warm. Serves 6–8.

SHRIMP JAMBALAYA

1/2 onion, minced
2 tbsp ham fat or lard
1 cup chopped cooked ham
2 tbsp flour
1 clove garlic, minced
2 lbs small cooked shrimp
2 cups canned or fresh tomatoes
    dash of cayenne pepper
1½ cups raw rice
1/2 tsp thyme
1/2 tsp marjoram
2 tsp chili powder
1 tsp ground cloves
1 tsp salt
1 cup cooked peas

Sauté onion in ham fat until transparent. Stir in flour until well blended. Add ham, garlic and shrimp. Cook, stirring frequently, until bubbly. Add the remaining ingredients except for peas and enough boiling water to moisten. Cook, covered, until rice is tender. Additional boiling water should be added as the moisture is absorbed. Just before serving, stir in peas. Serves 8.

BAKED CHEESE SANDWICH PIE

2	small eggs
1¼	cups flour
1/2	tsp salt
1/4	tsp pepper
1⅓	cups milk
1½	cups shredded Swiss, Cheddar or Muenster cheese

Preheat oven to 425°.
Combine eggs, flour, salt, pepper and milk in a bowl. Beat until smooth. Stir in 3/4 cup cheese. Pour into greased 9" round pan. Top with remaining cheese. Bake 30–35 min. until brown and puffy. Cut in wedges and serve immediately. Serves 6.

CHEESE AND SHRIMP SOUFFLÉ

12	slices of white bread
1/4	lb butter, softened
1	lb small cooked shrimp
1¼	lb grated mild Cheddar cheese
	salt and pepper to taste
6	eggs, beaten
3¼	cups milk
	paprika

Do *not* preheat oven.
Remove bread crusts and spread with butter. Cut into cubes. Grease a 2½-qt. casserole. Add alternate layers of bread cubes, shrimp and grated cheese, ending with cheese. Season each shrimp layer with salt and pepper to taste. Combine eggs and milk and pour into casserole so that liquid is just to the last layer. Sprinkle with paprika. Refrigerate at least 6 hr. or overnight. Bake at 350° for about 1 hr. or until soufflé is puffy and brown. Serves 8.

WILD RICE MOLD WITH SHRIMP

1	pkg (6-oz) wild, long-grain rice mix
1	tbsp butter
1/2	cup French Dressing (p. 120)
1/4	cup finely diced celery
1/4	cup finely diced green pepper
1/2	cup finely diced scallions
1/4	cup finely chopped parsley
1	lb cooked shrimp

Cook rice according to package directions. Add butter and stir until grains are covered. Pour rice into a colander, cover it with a cloth and set it over a pan of boiling water. Steam rice for 15 min. or until dry. Put rice in a bowl and allow to stand for 15 min. Add French Dressing and vegetables and mix. Pack tightly into a lightly oiled 4-cup ring mold or 6-8 individual molds and chill. Unmold on salad greens. Put shrimp in the center and serve with additional French Dressing. Serves 6–8.

NEW ORLEANS SHRIMP

3	tbsp butter
3	tbsp chopped onion
2	cups cooked shrimp, cut up
2	cups cooked rice
1½	cups sour cream
1/2	tsp salt
1/2	tsp celery salt
1/4	cup ketchup
	Garnish: pimiento

Melt butter and sauté onion until transparent. Add shrimp, rice, sour cream, salt, celery salt and ketchup. Heat gently over low heat until mixture is heated through. Do not boil. Serve garnished with thin strips of pimiento. Serves 6.

CURRIED SHRIMP AND CRABMEAT SALAD

2 pkg (6-oz) frozen crabmeat, thawed, drained and flaked
2 pkg (8-oz) frozen shrimp, cooked
2/3 cup mayonnaise
2 tbsp sour cream
1–2 tbsp curry powder
4 tsp minced onion
2 tsp minced parsley
2 tbsp dry sherry
2 tbsp lemon juice
1/4 cup ketchup
   Garnish: tomato and hard-boiled eggs

Place thawed crabmeat and cooked shrimp on paper towels and drain thoroughly. Combine the rest of the ingredients to make dressing. Mix in seafood and chill at least 3 hr. Serve salad on crisp greens garnished with tomato and hard-boiled egg wedges. Serves 6.

MOLDED SHRIMP AND CHEESE

2 tbsp unflavored gelatin
1/2 cup cold water
1 pkg (8-oz) cream cheese, cut in chunks
1 can (10¾-oz) tomato soup
2 lbs cooked shrimp, cut up
1 cup mayonnaise
2 tbsp lemon juice
1 tsp Worcestershire sauce
   dash of salt
1/4 cup chopped onion
3/4 cup chopped celery
2 tbsp chopped green pepper
1 tsp tarragon
2 pkg (10-oz) small frozen peas, cooked
   Garnish: hard-boiled egg and ripe olives

Soften gelatin in water for 5 min. Add cream cheese to tomato soup and heat, stirring until soup comes to a boil. Remove from heat and beat until smooth. Stir in gelatin until dissolved. Cool. Mix together shrimp, mayonnaise, lemon juice, Worcestershire, salt, onion, celery, green pepper and tarragon. Thoroughly combine with gelatin mixture. Pour into 2-qt. ring mold which has been rinsed in cold water. Chill until set. Unmold on salad greens. Fill center with buttered peas and garnish with slices of egg and ripe olive. May be serve with Russian Dressing (p. 119). Serves 8–10.

SHRIMP STRUDEL

1	pkg (8-oz) cream cheese, softened
1	cup sour cream
1	tsp salt
1	egg
1	lb cooked shrimp
2	tbsp chopped chives
1	lb sliced mushrooms
3	tbsp butter
8	filo pastry sheets (see directions p. 87)
	melted butter for brushing

Preheat oven to 375°.
Cream the cheese with sour cream. Add salt and beat in egg. Cut the shrimp into small pieces and add to cheese mixture, blending well. Add chives. Sauté mushrooms in butter. Butter a 8″ x 12″ shallow baking dish. Cover bottom and sides of baking dish with a whole filo sheet and brush with melted butter. Layer 3 more filo sheets into the dish, brushing each layer with butter. Spread mushrooms over filo evenly and top with shrimp mixture. Cover with 4 remaining filo sheets, brushing each sheet with butter. Turn down filo sides to seal. Brush top with butter. Bake about 40 min. or until top is golden brown. Serve piping hot. Serves 6–8.

EASY SHRIMP NEWBURG

     2 tbsp butter
   1/2 cup fresh mushrooms, sliced
     1 lb cooked shrimp
     1 can (10-oz) cream of shrimp soup
   1/4 cup milk
     2 tsp grated onion
   1/2 cup grated sharp Cheddar cheese
   1/4 cup dry sherry
     6 patty shells
        Garnish: parsley

Melt butter and sauté mushrooms and shrimp until mushrooms are tender. Add shrimp soup, milk, onion and cheese. Cook, stirring for about 5 min. until cheese is melted. Add sherry. Fill patty shells with shrimp mixture and garnish with parsley. Serves 6.

FAR EAST SHRIMP

     2 tbsp olive oil
     2 lbs raw shrimp, shelled and deveined
     1 small onion, chopped
   1/2 cup hot chicken broth
     1 can (8½-oz) thinly sliced water chestnuts, drained
     1 pkg (10-oz) frozen peas, thawed
   3/4 tsp powdered ginger
     1 tsp salt
     5 tsp flour
     2 tbsp cold water
     2 tbsp soy sauce
     2 tbsp dry sherry
        cooked rice
        assorted relishes

Heat oil in skillet. Add shrimp and onion. Cook, stirring until shrimp are pink or about 2 min. Add chicken broth, water chestnuts, peas, ginger and salt. Cover and cook until peas are tender or about 4 min. Make a paste by combining flour and water. Add paste, soy sauce and sherry to shrimp mixture. Cook, stirring over low heat until sauce has thickened. Serve over fluffy hot rice with assorted relishes. Serves 6.

SHRIMP WITH BÉARNAISE SAUCE

    1/4 cup butter
    1/2 lb chopped fresh mushrooms
      2 lbs cooked shrimp
      1 tbsp lemon juice
      1 tbsp minced parsley
    1/2 tsp nutmeg
         salt and pepper to taste
    1/4 cup tomato purée
    3/4 cup Béarnaise Sauce (p. 96)

Melt butter and sauté mushrooms and shrimp for 5 min. Add lemon juice, parsley, nutmeg, salt and pepper. Pile shrimp mixture into 6 individual baking shells or a 1½-qt. casserole. Combine tomato purée with the Béarnaise Sauce and spoon over the shrimp mixture. Place under broiler for 3–5 min. or until golden brown. Serves 6.

SHRIMP MOLD

      2 cans (1-pt) tomatoes
      1 pkg (6-oz) lemon-flavored gelatin
    1½   tsp lemon juice
         dash of salt
      1 tsp Worcestershire sauce
      1 tbsp horseradish
      1 lb small, cooked shrimp

Strain the tomatoes into a saucepan and reserve the pulp. Heat the juice, add the gelatin and stir until dissolved. Mix in the rest of the ingredients. Pour into a 5-cup ring mold or into 6 individual molds which have been rinsed in cold water and chill until firm. Unmold on salad greens. May be garnished with additional shrimp. Serves 6.

SALMON LOAF

1½ cups grated sharp Cheddar cheese
1 egg, beaten
3 tbsp milk
1 tbsp butter, melted
1/2 tsp salt
    dash of pepper
2 tbsp chopped parsley
1/2 cup fresh bread crumbs
2 cups cooked salmon, flaked

Preheat oven to 375°.
Thoroughly combine all ingredients. Shape into a loaf and place in greased 9" x 5" loaf pan. Cover top of loaf with additional buttered crumbs. Bake for about 40 min. or until crumbs are brown. May be served with Dill Sauce (p. 97). Serves 6.

SALMON MOUSSE

1 tbsp unflavored gelatin
1/4 cup cold water
1/2 cup boiling water
1/2 cup mayonnaise
1 tbsp lemon juice
1 tbsp minced onion
1 tbsp minced celery
1/2 tsp Tabasco sauce
1 tsp salt
2 cans (7¼-oz) red salmon
1/2 cup heavy cream, whipped
5 pitted ripe olives, sliced
2 hard-boiled eggs, sliced
    Dill Sauce (p. 97)

Soften gelatin in cold water for 5 min. Add boiling water and stir until dissolved. Cool. Add mayonnaise, lemon juice, onion, celery, Tabasco and salt. Mix thoroughly. Chill until just beginning to set. Drain and pick over salmon, removing skin and bones. Chop. Add to gelatin mixture. Fold in whipped cream. Decorate bottom and sides of a 6-cup fish mold which has been rinsed in cold water with sliced olives and hard-boiled eggs. Spoon mousse carefully into mold. Chill for at least 3 hr. Unmold on serving platter and serve with Dill Sauce. Serves 6–8.

DEVILED CRABMEAT

2	tbsp butter
1	tbsp chopped onion
2	tbsp chopped celery
2	tbsp flour
½	cup milk
½	cup cream
¼	tsp nutmeg
2	tsp prepared mustard
4	egg yolks
1/4	cup dry sherry
	salt and pepper to taste
3	pkg (6-oz) frozen crabmeat, thawed, drained and flaked
1½	cups mayonnaise

Preheat oven to 425°.
Melt butter and sauté onion and celery until onion is transparent. Stir in flour until well blended. Gradually add milk and cream, stirring constantly. Cook, stirring, over low heat until sauce just begins to thicken. Remove from heat and add nutmeg and mustard. Beat 2 egg yolks into 1/2 cup of the hot sauce. Pour back into saucepan and continue cooking until sauce is thickened and smooth. Stir in sherry, salt, pepper and crabmeat. Spoon the mixture into individual crab shells, ramekins or a 1½-qt. casserole. Combine mayonnaise with remaining 2 egg yolks and spread on top. Bake about 15 min. or until golden brown. Serves 6.

CRABMEAT MELON BOWL

1	large honeydew melon
2	pkg (6-oz) frozen crabmeat, thawed, drained and flaked
1½	cups thinly sliced celery
2	tbsp chopped parsley
1/2	lb baked or boiled ham slices, cut in strips
1/4	cup mayonnaise
2	tbsp lemon juice
1	tsp salt
1/4	tsp pepper
1	small cantaloupe melon, scooped into balls

Make a basket of the honeydew by cutting the top off about 1/4" down. Make balls of the melon meat and refrigerate. Completely scoop away insides. Cut a saw-toothed edge around top of melon with a sharp knife. Refrigerate melon basket. Mix crabmeat with celery, parsley and ham strips. Blend mayonnaise, lemon juice, salt and pepper. Toss crabmeat mixture with mayonnaise dressing. Pile lightly in melon basket and garnish with bits of crabmeat. Place basket on bed of lettuce and surround with melon balls. Serves 6–8.

GRILLED CRABMEAT SANDWICH

1	pkg (6-oz) frozen crabmeat, thawed, drained and flaked
1	pkg (8-oz) cream cheese, softened
2	tbsp butter, softened
2	tsp green onions, minced
6	English muffins, fork split
12	thin slices of tomato
12	thin slices of processed American cheese

Combine crabmeat, cream cheese, butter and onion. Spread mixture on English muffin halves. Top each with tomato slice and cheese slice that has been trimmed to fit. Place on cookie sheet and broil for 2–3 min. or until cheese has melted. Watch them carefully! Serves 6.

CRABMEAT MOUSSE
Blender

2	tbsp unflavored gelatin
2	tbsp dry sherry
1/2	cup chicken broth
2	eggs, separated
1	pkg (6-oz) frozen crabmeat, thawed, drained and flaked
5	drops Tabasco sauce
1	stalk celery, cut up
1	onion, sliced
2	tbsp chopped parsley
1/4	tsp marjoram
1	cup light cream

Pour gelatin, sherry and hot broth into blender and mix for a few seconds. Add the egg yolks, crabmeat, Tabasco, celery, onion, parsley and marjoram. Blend until smooth. Remove cover and with motor on, add cream. Beat the egg whites until stiff. Fold into crab mixture. Pour into a 4-cup mold which has been rinsed in cold water. Refrigerate until set or about 1½ hr. Serves 6.

CRABMEAT FONDUE

1/4	lb butter, softened
10	slices very thin bread, crusts removed
2	cups grated Cheddar cheese
2	pkg (6-oz) frozen crabmeat, thawed, drained and flaked
2	tsp sharp mustard
4	eggs, beaten
1	tsp salt
2¼	cups milk

Preheat oven to 350°.
Butter bread on both sides and cut into cubes. Place bread cubes in bottom of buttered 1½-qt. casserole. Cover with cheese and then crabmeat. Combine remaining ingredients and pour over crab mixture. Cover and refrigerate overnight or at least 8 hr. Bake for about 45 min. or until golden and puffy. Serves 6.

CRABMEAT AND MUSHROOM CASSEROLE

        3/4 lb chopped mushrooms
          6 small sweet gherkin pickles
        1/2 cup minced onion
          2 tbsp chopped parsley
          3 pkg (6-oz) frozen crabmeat, thawed, drained and flaked
          6 tbsp butter
          6 tbsp flour
       1½ cups milk
        1/2 cup light cream
        1/2 tsp salt
             pepper to taste
             dash of cayenne pepper
        1/2 cup dry sherry
        3/4 cup dry bread crumbs

Preheat oven to 350°.
Combine mushrooms, pickles, onions and parsley with crabmeat.
Melt butter, add flour and stir until well blended. Gradually add
milk and cream, stirring constantly. Cook, stirring, over low heat
until sauce is thickened and smooth. Remove from heat and add
seasonings and sherry. Combine sauce with crab mixture. Pour
into buttered 2-qt. casserole. Sprinkle with bread crumbs. Bake for
30 min. Serves 6–8.

CRABMEAT SURPRISE

          2 cups mayonnaise
          2 cups light cream
          1 pkg (8-oz) prepared, seasoned stuffing
          3 pkg (6-oz) frozen crabmeat, thawed, drained and flaked
          2 tbsp chopped parsley
          2 tbsp chopped onion
          3 hard-boiled eggs, chopped
        1/2 cup dry sherry

Preheat oven to 325°.

Combine mayonnaise and cream. Reserve 1/4 cup of seasoned stuffing to sprinkle on top. Combine the remaining stuffing with the rest of the ingredients and mix thoroughly. Place in a 2-qt. casserole. Sprinkle the 1/4 cup stuffing on top. Bake for 45 min. or until bubbly. Serves 6–8.

CRABMEAT-HAM-CHICKEN SOUFFLÉ

4	tbsp butter
4	tbsp flour
1¼	cups milk
1	tsp salt
1	tbsp Madeira wine
1	tbsp lemon juice
4	eggs, separated
1	pkg (6-oz) frozen crabmeat, thawed, drained and flaked
1	cup slivered ham
1	cup slivered chicken (white meat)
3/4	cup freshly grated Parmesan cheese

Preheat oven to 350°.

Melt butter and stir in flour until well blended. Gradually add milk, stirring constantly. Cook, stirring, over low heat until sauce is thickened and smooth. Add salt, Madeira and lemon juice. Lightly beat egg yolks. Stir half of the hot sauce into egg yolks, mixing well. Pour back into saucepan and stir to blend. Add crabmeat, ham and chicken. Beat egg whites until stiff and gently fold into crab mixture. Pour into a 2-qt. greased casserole. Sprinkle with Parmesan cheese. Place dish in pan of hot water and bake for 45 min. or until puffy and brown. Serves 6–8.

CRABMEAT DREAMS

16 thin slices of whole wheat bread
12 ounces cream cheese, softened
1/4 cup minced onion
2 pkg (6-oz) frozen crabmeat, thawed, drained and flaked
mayonnaise to moisten
1½ cups soft bread crumbs
1/2 cup butter, melted
16 slices of partially cooked bacon

Toast bread on one side. Combine cheese and onion and spread on untoasted side of bread. Moisten crabmeat with mayonnaise and spread this mixture over cheese. Mix bread crumbs with butter and sprinkle over crabmeat. Top each sandwich with a slice of bacon which has been halved. Put under broiler until crumbs are brown. Serves 8.

BAKED CLAMS WITH CHEESE

48 freshly opened clams on the half shell
1/3 cup minced green onions
3 tbsp dry white wine
1½ tbsp minced parsley
2 small cloves of garlic, minced
6 tbsp butter, softened
salt and freshly ground black pepper to taste
3 tbsp fine bread crumbs
48 1″ squares of Swiss cheese (about 1 lb)

Preheat oven to 400°.
Arrange the clams in one layer in a large baking dish or dishes. Combine onions and wine and boil until most of the liquid has evaporated. Cool. Combine parsley, garlic, butter, salt, pepper, bread crumbs, and the onion mixture. Spread a little of the butter mixture on each square of cheese. Place cheese, spread side down, on each clam. Bake about 8 min. Serves 6.

COQUILLES ST. JACQUES

1½	lbs deep sea scallops
1	cup white wine
1/2	cup water
3	tbsp butter
1	cup thinly sliced mushrooms
1	tbsp minced onion
1/2	cup buttered bread crumbs
1/2	cup freshly grated Parmesan cheese

MORNAY SAUCE

3	tbsp butter
3	tbsp flour
2/3	cup milk
1	cup scallop liquid
1/2	tsp salt
	dash of pepper
4	tbsp grated Swiss cheese
2	egg yolks, beaten
1/2	cup cream
2	tbsp dry sherry

Parboil scallops in wine and water for 5 min. until barely tender. Liquid should just cover scallops. Drain and reserve liquid. If liquid is more than 1 cup, reduce by boiling. Melt butter and sauté mushrooms and onions until onions are transparent.

MORNAY SAUCE: melt butter and stir in flour until well blended. Do not brown. Gradually add milk, scallop liquid, salt, pepper and pan juices from mushrooms and onion, stirring constantly. Cook, stirring until sauce is thickened and smooth. Stir in Swiss cheese. Mix egg yolks with cream and add a small amount of hot sauce. Add sherry and pour back into remaining sauce. Heat, but do not boil.

Add scallops, mushroom and onion. Fill 6 individual shells and top with buttered crumbs and Parmesan cheese. Place under broiler for 3–5 min. or until brown. Serves 6.

EGGPLANT AND CLAM CASSEROLE

                1   large eggplant
                2   cans (8-oz) minced clams
             1/4   cup minced onion
             1/4   cup butter
                3   tbsp flour
                2   cups light cream
             1/4   cup chopped parsley
             1/8   tsp garlic powder
             1/2   tsp salt
                     pepper to taste
                     dash of Tabasco sauce
                1   cup soft, buttered, bread crumbs

Preheat oven to 350°.
Peel and cut eggplant into pieces. Boil in a small amount of salted
water until tender. Drain well and mash. Drain clams, reserving
liquid. Combine clams with eggplant. Sauté onion in butter until
onion is transparent. Stir in flour until well blended. Gradually
add cream and reserved clam liquid, stirring constantly. Cook,
stirring over low heat until sauce is thickened and smooth. Add
eggplant, clam mixture, parsley and seasonings. Pour into a buttered 2-qt. casserole. Top with bread crumbs. Bake for about 30
min. Serves 8.

NICOISE SALAD

             DRESSING

                1   tsp garlic powder
                3   cans (7-oz) tuna fish, drained and flaked
                2   anchovy fillets, drained and chopped
                2   tsp chopped parsley
                1   tsp basil
                1   cup olive oil
             1/4   cup wine vinegar
            1½   tsp salt
                     freshly ground black pepper to taste

    2   qt lettuce, broken
 1/2   lb fresh cooked green beans, cut up
    2   hard-boiled eggs, sliced
    2   medium tomatoes, cut in thin slices
 1/2   medium green pepper, seeded and sliced
    4   green onions, chopped
    6   radishes, sliced
   12   pitted black olives
    4   mushrooms, sliced

Sprinkle garlic powder inside salad bowl. Reserve 1/4 cup tuna for garnish. Mix remaining tuna, anchovy, parsley, basil, oil, vinegar, salt and pepper in bowl to make the dressing. Refrigerate for about 1 hr. for flavors to blend. Place lettuce in salad bowl and artistically arrange vegetables. Pour dressing over all and garnish with remaining tuna. Bring to table before tossing for guests to view. Serves 6.

TUNA FISH SPAGHETTI SALAD

    1   pkg (8-oz) thin spaghetti
    3   cans (7-oz) tuna fish, drained and flaked
 1/2   pkg (10-oz) frozen peas, cooked until barely done
    1   carrot, finely chopped
    1   small onion, chopped
 1/3   cup mayonnaise
 1/3   cup sour cream
    1   tsp sugar
    1   tsp vinegar
 1/4   tsp fresh dill
  6–8 large tomatoes

Cook spaghetti until firm, according to instructions. Drain thoroughly and cut into small pieces. Combine with tuna, peas, carrot and onion. Make a dressing by blending together the mayonnaise, sour cream, sugar, vinegar and fresh dill. Lightly toss with tuna mixture until coated. Refrigerate, covered, for several hours. Hollow out tomatoes and fill with salad. Arrange on lettuce shells. Serves 6–8.

AVOCADO AND TUNA FISH MOLD

AVOCADO LAYER

1	tbsp unflavored gelatin
2/3	cup water
1	large avocado
1/4	cup lemon juice
1/2	cup sour cream
1/2	cup mayonnaise
1	tsp salt
1/8	tsp Tabasco sauce

AVOCADO LAYER: soften gelatin in water for 5 min. Cook over low heat until gelatin is dissolved. Refrigerate until mixture is just beginning to set. Peel and mash avocado and combine with remaining ingredients. Stir in gelatin. Pour into 9" x 5" loaf pan which has been rinsed with a little lemon juice. Chill until set.

TUNA FISH LAYER

1	tbsp unflavored gelatin
1¼	cups water
1/3	cup lemon juice
1	tsp Worcestershire sauce
1	tsp salt
1	can (7-oz) tuna fish (crabmeat, shrimp or lobster)
1	cup diced celery
1/3	cup diced pimiento
	Garnish: tomatoes, ripe olives and avocado

TUNA FISH LAYER: soften gelatin in 1/2 cup water. Cook over low heat until gelatin dissolves. Add lemon juice, Worcestershire sauce, salt and the remaining water. Cover and refrigerate until mixture is just beginning to set. Fold in the remaining ingredients. Pour on top of avocado layer. Cover and chill until firm. Unmold on serving platter and garnish with tomato wedges, ripe olive and avocado slices. Serves 6.

BAKED TUNA FISH LOAF

- 1/2 cup milk
- 2 eggs, beaten
- 2 cups soft bread crumbs
- 1/4 cup freshly grated Parmesan cheese
- 1 tbsp minced parsley
- 1/4 tsp pepper
- 1/4 cup minced onion
- 3 cans (7-oz) tuna fish, drained and flaked
  Garnish: lemon

Preheat oven to 350°.
Combine milk, eggs, bread crumbs, cheese, parsley, pepper and onion. Stir until thoroughly blended. Mix tuna into egg mixture. Line a 9" x 5" loaf pan with greased foil. Pour tuna mixture into it. Bake for 45 min. Lift out of pan and pull down foil from sides. Carefully lift loaf off foil with wide spatula. Garnish with lemon slices. Loaf may be serve with Quick Parsley Sauce (p. 97). Serves 6.

TUNA FISH INDIENNE

- 1/2 cup mayonnaise
- 1/4 cup cream cheese, softened
- 1½ tsp curry powder
  dash of pepper
- 1 tbsp lemon juice
- 1 can (7-oz) tuna fish
- 1/2 cup minced celery
- 1/4 cup slivered almonds, toasted
- 1/2 cup shredded coconut
- 6 slices of bread, toasted on one side

Combine mayonnaise, cream cheese, curry powder, pepper and lemon juice. Thoroughly mix in tuna, celery, almonds and coconut. Pile mixture on untoasted side of bread and broil for 3–5 min. or until bubbly and brown. Serves 6.

TUNA FISH SOUFFLÉ RING

        3   eggs, separated
        2   cans (7-oz) tuna fish, drained and flaked
        1   can (10¾-oz) cream of mushroom soup
      1/2   cup fine cracker crumbs
      1/4   cup minced onion
        2   tbsp chopped parsley
        2   tbsp diced pimiento
        1   tbsp lemon juice

Preheat oven to 350°.
Lightly beat the egg yolks. Thoroughly combine with tuna, soup,
crumbs, onion, parsley, pimiento and lemon juice. Beat the egg
whites until stiff and fold into tuna mixture. Pour into a greased
5-cup ring mold. Bake for 30 min. Turn out on serving plate.
Cooked peas may be served in the center of the ring. Serves 8.

HOT CHEESE AND TUNA FISH SANDWICH

        2   cans (7-oz) tuna fish, drained and flaked
      1/2   cup chopped celery
            mayonnaise to moisten
        1   tsp Worcestershire sauce
        1   tsp lemon juice
            salt and pepper to taste
        6   hamburger rolls, halved
       12   slices of American cheese

Combine tuna, celery, mayonnaise, Worcestershire sauce, lemon
juice, salt and pepper. Spread on hamburger rolls. Top each with
a slice of cheese, trimmed to fit. Place on a cookie sheet and broil
for 2–3 min. until the cheese has melted. Watch them carefully!
Serves 6.

CREAMY CHICKEN SALAD

- 1/2 cup mayonnaise
- 2½ tsp sugar
- 2½ tsp vinegar
  - salt and pepper to taste
- 3/4 cup heavy cream, whipped
- 1 cup chopped celery
- 3 cups cooked chicken, diced
- 3 large ripe avocados
- 2 tsp lemon juice
- 1/2 cup chopped cashew nuts

Combine mayonnaise with sugar, vinegar, salt and pepper. Gently fold in whipped cream. Fold in celery and chicken. Cover and refrigerate until well chilled. To serve: peel and cut avocados in half, lengthwise. Remove pits and sprinkle with lemon juice to prevent discoloration. Mound salad on top of each avocado half and sprinkle with cashews. Serve on salad greens. Serves 6.

CURRIED CHICKEN SALAD WITH FRUIT

- 3 cups cooked chicken, diced
- 1 cup chopped celery
- 1 tsp salt
- 2 tbsp lemon juice
- 1 cup green seedless grapes, halved
- 1 can (11-oz) mandarin oranges, drained
- 1 cup mayonnaise
- 2 tsp curry powder
- 1 tbsp soy sauce
  - Garnish: slivered almonds, toasted

Combine chicken, celery, salt and lemon juice. Add 1/2 cup grapes and half of the mandarin oranges to chicken mixture. Combine mayonnaise, curry powder and soy sauce to make salad dressing. Toss dressing with chicken and fruit mixture. Refrigerate for at least 2 hr. Serve on salad greens garnished with almonds and remaining oranges and grapes. Serves 6.

CHICKEN AND SOUR CREAM MOUSSE

        2   tbsp unflavored gelatin
      1/2   cup cold water
        1   can (13¾-oz) chicken broth (1¾ cups)
        3   tbsp lemon juice
        1   tsp dry mustard
        1   tbsp curry powder
        2   tsp grated onion
        2   cups sour cream
        3   cups cooked chicken, diced
        1   cup minced celery
      1/4   cup minced apple
      1/4   cup slivered almonds, toasted
            Garnish: water cress, cherry tomatoes *or* grapes and man-
            darin oranges

Soften gelatin in cold water for 5 min. Heat chicken broth, add
gelatin and stir until dissolved. Remove from heat. Add lemon
juice, mustard, curry and onion. Let cool for 5 min. Mix in sour
cream. Cover and refrigerate until mixture just begins to set. Fold
in chicken, celery, apple and almonds. Pour into 1½-qt. mold
which has been rinsed with cold water. Refrigerate at least 4 hr.
or until firm. Unmold on water cress and serve with cherry
tomatoes *or* grapes and mandarin oranges. Serves 8–10.

ORANGE CHEF'S SALAD

        3   cups water cress
        3   cups lettuce
        2   cups orange sections
      1½   cups diced, unpeeled apple
        2   cups cooked chicken, chopped
      3/4   cup sharp Cheddar cheese, diced
        1   cup Sweet French Dressing (p. 120)

Wash and crisp salad greens and tear into pieces. Combine
greens, orange, apple, chicken and cheese. Toss lightly with dressing. Serves 6.

CHICKEN-SAUSAGE-MUSHROOM PIE

FILLING

1/2	lb sausage meat
12	large mushroom caps, sliced
1/4	cup plus 1 tbsp. butter
1/4	cup flour
1	tsp salt
	pepper to taste
2	cups chicken broth
2/3	cup light cream
2	cups cooked chicken, cut up

PASTRY

1/3	cup margarine
1	cup sifted flour
1/2	tsp salt
1	tsp celery seed
3/4	tsp paprika
2	tbsp water

Preheat oven to 425°.

FILLING: form sausage into small balls and sauté until brown. Drain fat and sauté the mushroom caps in 1 tbsp. butter. Melt remaining 1/4 cup butter and stir in flour, salt and pepper until well blended. Gradually add chicken broth and cream, stirring constantly. Cook, stirring, over low heat until sauce is thickened and smooth. Divide sausage, mushroom and chicken among 6 individual baking dishes. Pour hot sauce over each. Top with pastry.

PASTRY: cut margarine into a mixture of flour and salt until it is the consistency of coarse meal. Add celery seed and paprika. Add 2 tbsp. water and mix well with a fork until pastry holds together. Roll out pastry on a floured board to make a thin crust. Cut in circles the size of the baking dish. Cover each dish and prick pastry. Bake for 30–35 min. Serves 6.

CHICKEN SOUFFLÉ

6	tbsp butter
6	tbsp flour
2	cups milk
4	eggs, separated
3	cups cooked chicken, diced
1	tbsp dry sherry
1	tsp tarragon
3/4	tsp Worcestershire sauce
	salt and pepper to taste
1/4	cup cracker or dry bread crumbs

Preheat oven to 325°.
Melt 3 tbsp. butter and stir in flour until well blended. Gradually add the milk, stirring constantly. Cook, stirring, over low heat until the sauce is thickened and smooth. Remove from heat and stir half of the hot sauce into the beaten egg yolks, mixing well. Pour egg mixture back into saucepan, stirring. Add chicken and continue cooking for a minute longer. Add sherry, tarragon, Worcestershire sauce, salt and pepper. Beat egg white until stiff and gently fold into the chicken mixture. Pour into a buttered 2-qt. soufflé or baking dish. Sprinkle top with crumbs and dot with remaining butter. Set dish in pan of warm water and bake for 25–30 min. or until puffed and brown. Serve soufflé immediately. Serves 6.

MUSHROOM-STUFFED CHICKEN BREASTS

FILLING

3	tbsp butter
1	tbsp minced onion
2	tbsp minced celery
1/2	lb sliced mushrooms
1/2	tsp salt
	dash of pepper
1	tbsp lemon juice
1/3	cup slivered almonds, toasted

    1½   tbsp flour
     4   whole chicken breasts
     3   tbsp butter, melted
     2   cups crushed potato chips
    1/2 lb whole mushrooms

Preheat oven to 350°.

FILLING: melt butter and sauté onion, celery and mushroom until onion is transparent. Thoroughly mix in remaining filling ingredients.

Bone and skin chicken breasts. Cut them in half and pound until flat. Place a spoonful of mushroom filling on each chicken piece. Roll carefully, tucking in the sides, and secure with a toothpick. Combine butter and crushed potato chips. Coat chicken with butter mixture. Bake covered for 45 min. Uncover and add whole mushrooms. Bake 15 min. longer or until chicken is done. Serves 8.

CHICKEN SANDWICH SOUFFLÉ

    12   slices of thin sliced bread, crusts removed
     3   cups cooked chicken, chopped
     6   slices of Swiss cheese
     3   small eggs, beaten
    1½   cups undiluted cream of chicken soup
    1/2 tsp salt
     2   tbsp chopped onion
    3/4 tsp dry mustard
     1   tbsp fresh lemon juice
    1/3 cup chopped pimiento
    1/2 cup milk

Preheat oven to 350°.

Grease a 8" x 12" shallow baking dish. Place 6 slices of bread on the bottom of the dish. Top with chicken, Swiss cheese and 6 slices of bread. Combine remaining ingredients and beat well. Pour sauce over sandwiches and bake for 40 min. or until golden and puffy. Serves 6.

CHICKEN SALAD MANDALAY

2/3	cup raisins
1/2	cup white wine
3	cups cooked chicken, cubed
2/3	cup shredded coconut
2/3	cup peanuts
1½	cups mayonnaise
1/2	cup chopped chutney
1	avocado
1	banana

Soak raisins in wine for about 1 hr. Drain and combine with chicken, coconut, peanuts, mayonnaise and chutney. Chill thoroughly. To serve: peel and dice avocado and slice banana. Add to salad mixture. Serve on crisp salad greens. Serves 6.

MUSHROOMS STUFFED WITH CHICKEN LIVERS IN WINE SAUCE

24	very large mushrooms
1/4	lb butter, melted
	salt and pepper to taste
1	lb chicken livers
6	thin slices of white bread, toasted

WINE SAUCE

2	green onions, sliced
1	cup dry white wine
4	tbsp butter
4	tbsp flour
1	can (13¾-oz) chicken broth (1¾ cups)
1½	tbsp lemon juice
1½	tbsp chopped parsley

Remove stems and sauté mushroom caps in 4 tbsp. of the butter until tender. Add salt and pepper to taste. Remove from pan. Add remaining butter and sauté chicken livers over high heat for about 5 min. stirring often. Remove from pan and chop. Fill mushroom caps with the chopped liver. Cut toast into triangles and place 2 filled mushroom caps on each triangle.

WINE SAUCE: simmer onions in wine until the liquid is reduced in half. Melt butter and stir in flour until well blended. Gradually add the chicken broth and onion mixture, stirring constantly. Cook, stirring over low heat until sauce is thickened and smooth. Add lemon juice and parsley.

Pour Wine Sauce over stuffed mushroom caps and serve immediately. Serves 6.

CHICKEN AND HAM IN BÉCHAMEL SAUCE

1/4	cup flour
1/2	tsp salt
	dash of pepper
1/4	tsp nutmeg
1/2	tsp dry mustard
1/4	cup butter
1	cup chicken broth
1½	cups light cream
2	egg yolks, beaten
2	tsp grated lemon rind
1½	cups cooked chicken, cut in chunks
1	cup cooked ham, cut in chunks
6	patty shells or toast points

Combine flour, salt, pepper, nutmeg and mustard. Melt butter and stir in flour mixture well blended. Gradually add chicken broth and cream, stirring constantly. Cook, stirring, over low heat until sauce is thickened and smooth. Remove from heat. Stir half of the sauce into the egg yolks, mixing well. Pour back into saucepan. Cook, stirring about 2 min. longer. Mix in grated lemon rind, chicken and ham. Heat thoroughly. Serve in patty shells or on toast points. Serves 6.

HOT CHICKEN SALAD

         2 cups cooked chicken, diced
    1 ½ cups chopped celery
         3 tbsp chopped onion
    1/2 tsp salt
    1/2 tsp tarragon
         1 tsp Worcestershire sauce
    1/2 cup slivered almonds, toasted
         2 tbsp lemon juice
         1 cup mayonnaise
         1 cup Chinese fried noodles
    1/3 cup freshly grated Parmesan cheese

Preheat oven to 350°.
Combine chicken, celery, onion, salt, tarragon, Worcestershire
sauce, almonds, lemon juice and mayonnaise in a 2-qt. casserole.
Top with fried noodles and sprinkle with Parmesan cheese. Bake
for about 30 min. or until heated through. Serves 6.

DEVONSHIRE SANDWICHES

         6 slices of bread, toasted
       18 thin slices of chicken or turkey breast
       18 slices of bacon, crisply cooked
    1/2 cup freshly grated Parmesan cheese

         CHEESE SAUCE

    1/4 cup butter
    1/4 cup bacon fat
    2/3 cup flour
         3 cups milk
    3/4 lb grated sharp Cheddar cheese
    1/2 tsp sage
    1 ½ tsp dry mustard
         salt and pepper to taste

82   ENTRÉES

Place toast slices in a large flat baking dish. Top with chicken and bacon. Prepare sauce.

CHEESE SAUCE: melt butter and bacon fat and stir in flour until well blended. Gradually add milk, stirring constantly. Cook, stirring over low heat until sauce is thickened and smooth. Add Cheddar cheese, sage, mustard, salt and pepper, mixing until cheese melts. Spoon sauce over the chicken and sprinkle with Parmesan cheese. Broil for 2-3 min. or until top is golden brown. Serves 6.

TURKEY AND CHEESE SANDWICHES

12	slices of bread
3	eggs, beaten
3/4	cup milk
1/2	tsp salt
2	tbsp butter
1	can (10½-oz) cream of mushroom soup
1/2	cup heavy cream
1/2	cup chicken broth
1	tsp ketchup
1	tbsp dry sherry
	pepper to taste
2	cups cooked turkey, diced
2/3	cup grated Cheddar cheese

Preheat oven to 350°.

Dip bread slices into mixture of eggs, milk, and salt. Melt butter and sauté bread on both sides. Combine soup, cream, broth, ketchup, sherry, pepper and turkey. Arrange 6 slices of bread in shallow baking dish. Spoon turkey mixture on top of each. Cover with the remaining 6 bread slices. Sprinkle with cheese and bake for 15 min. Serves 6.

WATERMELON BASKET

    1   watermelon
        fresh fruit including apple, melon, berries, peaches, oranges, grapefruit, grapes, pineapple, bananas
    1   cup sugar
    1   cup white wine or light rum

Make a basket with a handle out of the watermelon. Placing the melon lengthwise, cut a basket handle from the top one-third of the melon. The remaining two-thirds of the melon becomes the basket when you scoop out the fruit. Scoop the pulp out carefully and save the good pieces for making melon balls. Cut "saw teeth" around the edge of the basket with a sharp knife. Refrigerate basket.

Cut up fruits and make melon balls, using enough fruit to fill basket. Combine fruit with sugar, wine or rum. Mix gently. Refrigerate for at least 3 hr. To serve: fill basket with well-drained fruit and place on a serving platter surrounded by salad greens. Fruit salad may be served with Ruby Salad Dressing (p. 119). Flowers may be tied to the handle of the basket for decoration. Basket may be made the day before. Serves 10.

TOMATO ASPIC CAROUSEL

    ASPIC

    2   tbsp unflavored gelatin
1/2   cup cold water
1½   cups tomato juice
1/2   cup white wine
    1   tsp salt
    1   tsp confectioners' sugar
    1   bay leaf
    1   small onion, chopped
        dash of cayenne pepper
        dash of celery salt
        strip of lemon rind

GARNISHES

12–15   baby carrots, turnips, new potatoes, scallions, radishes, and
      celery strips
  1   cup peas
  1   cup lima beans
     French Dressing (p. 120).

HAM ROLLS

1/4   cup chopped walnuts
  1   pkg (3-oz) cream cheese, softened
  8   thin slices of ham
    water cress

ASPIC: Soften gelatin in water for 5 min. Combine remaining ingredients and simmer for 15 min. Strain and add gelatin mixture, stirring until dissolved. Pour into 3-cup ring mold which has been rinsed with cold water. Cover and chill until firm.

GARNISHES: cut carrots and turnips into pieces and cook with potato, peas and lima beans. Let cool and toss with French Dressing. Cut radishes into roses. Soak radishes, celery strips and scallions in ice water.

HAM ROLLS: combine walnuts and cream cheese. Spread on ham slices and roll like a jelly roll.

Unmold salad on large plain platter. Surround with small mounds of vegetables, alternating the various kinds. Place ham rolls and water cress in center of ring mold and serve salad with extra French Dressing. Serves 6.

MOUSSAKA

       3   medium eggplants
     1/2   cup margarine
     1/4   cup olive oil
       3   large onions, finely chopped
       2   lbs ground lamb or beef
       3   tbsp tomato paste
     1/2   cup red wine
     1/3   cup chopped parsley
     3/4   tsp cinnamon
           salt and pepper to taste
     1/2   cup butter
       6   tbsp flour
       4   cups milk
       4   eggs, beaten
       2   cups cottage cheese
     1/2   tsp nutmeg
       1   cup dry bread crumbs
       1   cup freshly grated Parmesan cheese

Preheat oven to 350°.
Peel and slice eggplant in 1/2"slices. Brown slices quickly in 1/2
cup of margarine. Set aside. Add olive oil to pan. Sauté onions
until they are transparent. Add meat and cook until brown. Combine tomato paste, wine, parsley, cinnamon, salt and pepper. Add
to meat and simmer until liquid has been absorbed.
Melt butter and stir in flour until well blended. Gradually add milk,
stirring constantly. Cook, stirring over low heat until sauce is thickened and smooth. Remove from heat and stir in beaten eggs,
cottage cheese and nutmeg.
Grease an 11" x 16" pan. Sprinkle bottom lightly with bread
crumbs. Arrange alternate layers of eggplant and meat mixture,
sprinkling each layer with Parmesan cheese and bread crumbs.
Pour cheese mixture over all and bake 1 hr. and 10 min. or until
top is golden. Cool about 1/2 hr. before serving. Moussaka should
be made a day in advance to allow the flavors to blend. To reheat,
cover with foil and warm at 300° for about 30 min. Serves 10.

GREEK MEAT PIE

1	lb ground lamb
1	lb ground beef
1	onion, minced
2	tbsp olive oil
1	tsp oregano
1	tsp salt
	pepper to taste
1/3	cup tomato sauce
2	eggs, slightly beaten
1/2	cup freshly grated Parmesan cheese
1/4	lb butter, melted
12	filo pastry sheets

Preheat oven to 350°.

Sauté the lamb, beef and onion in oil. Season with oregano, salt and pepper. Add tomato sauce and cook until sauce is absorbed. Remove from heat and stir in eggs and cheese. Lightly butter a 8" x 12" shallow baking dish.

Filo preparation: any dish made with filo dough brings forth the most lavish praise from guests. It is not difficult to work with once you become accustomed. to handling the strudel-like pastry sheets. The pastry may be purchased in most stores selling gourmet items or specialty shops featuring Greek or Near Eastern foods. Keep filo dough frozen until ready to use. Remove from freezer the night before using, and refrigerate. Lay a damp towel on working surface and cover with a piece of wax paper. Add the desired number of filo sheets; cover with a piece of wax paper and a second damp towel. This prevents the dough from drying while you work. Proceed as directed in the recipe.

Cover bottom and sides of baking dish with a whole filo sheet and brush with butter. Layer 5 more filo sheets into the dish, brushing each layer with butter. Spread the meat mixture evenly over the filo. Cover with 6 remaining filo sheets, brushing each with butter. Turn down filo sides to seal. Brush top with butter. Before baking, cut in serving pieces just through top layers of filo. Bake about 40–45 min. or until top is golden brown. Serve hot or cold. Serves 8–10.

RUSSIAN MEAT PIE

PASTRY

1½   cups sifted flour
1/8   tsp salt
1/4   cup butter
1/4   cup shortening
1/3   cup cold water

Preheat oven to 400°.
Mix the flour and salt. Cut in butter and shortening with pastry blender or fingers until the consistency of coarse meal. Add water and mix with a fork to form a ball. Do not overwork dough. Divide dough in half. Roll out bottom crust and fit into a 10" pie plate.

FILLING

2   tbsp butter
1   large onion, chopped
1½   lbs ground round steak
2   tbsp flour
3/4   cup beef broth
2   hard-boiled eggs, sieved
3   tbsp horseradish
1/8   tsp salt
1   tsp pepper
1   tsp dill weed
1   egg yolk
1   tbsp water

Melt butter and sauté onion until transparent. Add the meat and cook until just brown. Remove from heat and sprinkle with flour and beef broth. Mix in the eggs and seasonings. Fill pie shell with meat mixture. Roll out remaining dough to make a top crust. Cover pie and carefully crimp the edges to seal. Thoroughly prick the pastry. Combine the egg yolk and water and brush the top of the pie. Bake for 30–35 min. or until crust is brown. Serves 8.

VEAL AND HAM ROLLS

12	thin slices of ham
12	very thin slices of veal
3	tsp sage
1/2	cup fresh bread crumbs
1/2	cup flour
1/4	cup butter
1/4	cup olive oil
	salt and pepper to taste
3/4	cup white wine

Place a slice of ham on each piece of veal and pound to press the two together. Sprinkle 1/4 tsp. sage on top of each. Roll the slices as a jelly roll and tie securely with a string. Combine crumbs and flour and dredge the meat rolls in the mixture. Heat butter and oil in a skillet and brown rolls on all sides. Season with salt and pepper. Add wine. Cover and cook over low heat for 10 min. Turn the rolls once. Serves 6.

MELON AND COLD MEAT PLATTER

1	cantaloupe melon
1	honeydew melon
1	fresh pineapple
2	lbs sliced cold meats (prosciutto, ham, smoked tongue, roast beef, Lebanon bologna)
1	pkg (8-oz) cream cheese, softened
	Sweet French Dressing (p. 120)
	Garnish: water cress

Peel melons and pineapple. Cut into wedges and arrange in the center of a platter. Fill some slices of cold meat with cream cheese or water cress and shape into cornucopias. Fold other meat slices into triangles or small rolls. Place the meat decoratively around the cantaloupe and pineapple wedges. Garnish lavishly with water cress and serve accompanied with Sweet French Dressing. Serves 6.

CORNED BEEF IN ASPIC

2	tbsp unflavored gelatin
1/2	cup cold water
1	can (13¾-oz) beef broth (1¾ cups)
1/2	cup Madeira wine
1/4	cup tomato juice
1	tsp Worcestershire sauce
2	tsp lemon juice
	dash of Tabasco sauce
1/3	lb corned beef (or roast beef), thinly sliced
1½	cups dill pickles, cut in thin strips
3	hard-boiled eggs, sliced
2	tbsp capers
	Garnish: water cress and ripe olives

Soften gelatin in cold water for 5 min. Heat broth, add gelatin and stir until dissolved. Add wine, tomato juice, Worcestershire sauce, lemon juice and Tabasco sauce. Cool. Pour a 1/4" layer of aspic into the bottom of a 9" x 5" loaf pan which has been rinsed with cold water. Chill until mixture just begins to set. Artistically arrange one-third the amount of beef, pickles, eggs and capers on the aspic layer. Cover with one-fourth of remaining aspic mixture. Cover and chill until it just begins to set. Continue layers twice more, ending with aspic. Chill until firm. Unmold on platter and garnish with water cress and ripe olive slices. May be served with Horseradish Dressing (p. 123). Serves 6.

PINEAPPLE HAM LOAF

1/4	cup light brown sugar, packed
1-1¼	cups pineapple chunks, drained
	cloves
2	eggs, beaten
1	can (10½-oz) cream of mushroom soup
1/4	cup ketchup
1/4	cup water
1	lb ground cooked ham

    1   lb ground veal
    1   cup dry bread crumbs
  1/2   tsp salt
        pepper to taste
    1   onion, minced
    3   tbsp minced green pepper

Preheat oven to 350°.
Grease a 9" x 5" loaf pan and sprinkle pan with the brown sugar. Stick pineapple chunks with clove and place, clove side down, to cover the bottom of the pan. Combine eggs, soup, ketchup and water. Thoroughly mix remaining ingredients. Pack on top of pineapple in pan. Bake for about 1 hr. Remove from oven and invert on serving platter. May be served hot or cold with Fluffy Mustard Sauce (p. 98). Serves 8–10.

CHEESE, HAM AND BROCCOLI FONDUE

    7   slices of white bread
    2   tbsp butter
  1/2   lb grated sharp Cheddar cheese
    1   pkg (10-oz) frozen chopped broccoli, cooked and drained
  1½   cups baked ham, diced
    5   eggs, beaten
    3   cups milk
    2   tbsp grated onion
  1/2   tsp salt
  1/2   tsp dry mustard

Make a doughnut from each bread slice by using two different sized round cutters. Butter doughnut and hole pieces and set aside. Place the crusts and scraps of bread in the bottom of a 8" x 12" casserole. Sprinkle cheese over the bread, add a layer of broccoli, then ham. Arrange doughnuts and holes on top. Combine remaining ingredients and pour over. Cover and refrigerate at least 6 hr. or overnight. Preheat oven to 325° and bake uncovered for about 50 min. or until set and brown. Remove from oven and allow to sit 10 min. before serving. Serves 6.

HAM AND ASPARAGUS WITH EGG SAUCE

6   slices of baked ham
3   tbsp butter
12 toast triangles
30 cooked asparagus spears

EGG SAUCE

6   tbsp butter
2   tsp minced onion
1/2 cup chopped mushrooms
6   tbsp flour
1   cup milk
1   cup light cream
     salt and pepper to taste
1/4 tsp nutmeg
1/3 cup freshly grated Parmesan cheese
3   hard-boiled eggs, sliced
     Garnish: pimiento

Sauté ham slices in butter until heated. Place a slice of ham on 2 toast triangles and top with 5 hot asparagus spears. Prepare sauce.

EGG SAUCE: melt butter and sauté onion and mushrooms until onion is transparent. Stir in flour until well blended. Gradually add milk and cream, stirring constantly. Cook, stirring over low heat until sauce is thickened and smooth. Season with salt, pepper and nutmeg. Add cheese and stir until melted. Gently stir in egg slices.

Spoon sauce over the asparagus and ham and garnish with strips of pimiento. Serves 6.

HAM AND CORN CUSTARD

1   pkg (10-oz) frozen corn (sweet white corn)
    salt and pepper to taste
1   tbsp sugar

          2   cups coarse bread crumbs
          3   tbsp butter
          2   cups cooked ham, minced
          2   eggs, beaten
       1½   cups milk
          1   tbsp prepared mustard

Preheat oven to 350°.

Cook corn according to package directions. Drain and add salt, pepper and sugar. Put half the corn in the bottom of a buttered 2-qt. casserole. Cover with one-third of the bread crumbs, dot with 1 tbsp. butter and add half of the ham. Repeat the layers, ending with crumbs and butter on top. Mix eggs, milk and mustard and pour over casserole. Bake for about 30 min. or until custard is firm and a knife inserted into the center comes out clean. Serves 6.

HAM MEATBALLS ON PINEAPPLE ROUNDS

          1   lb ground smoked ham
       1½   lbs ground lean pork
       1/4   cup milk
          1   egg, beaten
          1   cup plus 3 tbsp light brown sugar, packed
       1/2   cup white vinegar
       1/2   cup water
       1/2   tsp dry mustard
          2   tbsp butter, melted
       6–8   pineapple slices

Preheat oven to 350°.

Thoroughly mix the ground ham, pork, milk and egg. Shape into meatballs 1–1½" in diameter. Place in one layer in a shallow baking pan. Combine 1 cup of the brown sugar, vinegar, water and mustard. Pour over meatballs. Bake uncovered for 1 hr. Baste several times while baking. Meanwhile, combine the butter and 3 tbsp. of brown sugar and spread on the pineapple. Just before serving place the pineapple slices under the broiler for 1–2 min. until glazed. Serve meatballs over pineapple slices and spoon the sauce over each serving. Serves 6–8.

HAM TIMBALES WITH MUSHROOM SAUCE

       1/4   cup butter
         1   cup soft bread crumbs
         1   tbsp chopped onion
         1   tbsp chopped parsley
         1   cup scalded milk
       2½   cups cooked ham, cubed (or crabmeat, chicken, lobster)
         4   eggs
         2   tbsp dry sherry
              salt and pepper to taste
              Mushroom Sauce (p. 96)

Preheat oven to 350°.
Melt butter and add bread crumbs, onion and parsley. Cook until
crumbs are a light brown. Stir in milk and cook over low heat for
5 min. stirring often. Add ham and eggs that have been beaten
with the sherry, salt and pepper. Divide mixture into 6 individual
1-cup molds, which have been buttered. Fill them about two-
thirds full. Set molds in pan of hot water and bake for 25–30 min.
or until a knife inserted into the center comes out clean. Cool for
2 or 3 min. before unmolding on a round serving platter. Serve
with Mushroom Sauce. Serves 6.

HAM AND SWISS CHEESE SANDWICHES

        12   slices of bread, crusts removed
       1/2   lb thinly sliced ham
       3/4   lb thinly sliced Swiss cheese
         3   eggs, beaten
              salad oil for frying

Make 6 ham and Swiss cheese sandwiches, placing a ham slice
folded in half between slices of Swiss cheese. Cut sandwiches in
half. Dip each half in egg and then fry in about 1½" of hot oil for
5–8 min. or until completely puffed and golden. Keep the sandwiches warm in the oven until ready to serve. Serves 6.

HAM CASSEROLE SUPREME

6 tbsp butter
2½ cups chopped cooked ham steak
1 cup chopped onion
3/4 lb mushrooms
2 cups fresh bread crumbs
1 tsp thyme
1/4 tsp sage
  salt and pepper to taste
2 cups sour cream

Preheat oven to 350°.
Melt 3 tbsp. butter and sauté ham until heated through. Melt remaining butter and sauté onion until transparent. Finely chop mushrooms and sauté with onion until juices have evaporated. Add to ham. Mix together bread crumbs, thyme, sage, salt and pepper. Combine 1½ cups seasoned bread crumbs with sour cream and ham mixture. Pour into greased 1½ qt. baking dish. Top with remaining bread crumbs. Bake for 20 min. or until crumbs are golden. Serves 6.

CHEESE SAUCE

3 tbsp butter
3 tbsp flour
1½ cups milk
1½ cups grated sharp Cheddar cheese
1/4 cup chopped pimiento
1/2 tsp dry mustard
1/2 tsp salt
  dash of cayenne pepper

Melt butter and stir in flour until well blended. Gradually add milk, stirring constantly. Cook, stirring over low heat until thickened and smooth. Add cheese, pimiento and seasonings. Yield: 3 cups.

BÉARNAISE SAUCE
Blender

2 tbsp white wine
1 tbsp tarragon vinegar
1 tsp tarragon
2 tsp chopped onion
1/4 tsp pepper
1/2 cup butter
3 egg yolks
2 tbsp lemon juice
1/4 tsp salt
dash of cayenne pepper

Combine wine, vinegar, tarragon, onion and pepper in a small skillet. Bring to a boil and cook until liquid disappears. Set aside. Heat the butter to bubbling. Do not brown. Pour herb mixture, egg yolks, lemon juice, salt and cayenne into blender. With motor on low speed, gradually add hot butter and blend until sauce is thickened and smooth. Yield: 1 cup.

MUSHROOM SAUCE

2 tbsp butter
3/4 lb mushrooms, thinly sliced
1 small onion, chopped
1 tbsp chopped parsley
1/2 tsp garlic powder
salt and pepper to taste
1½ tbsp flour
1 cup chicken broth
1/4 cup dry sherry

Melt butter and sauté mushrooms for 5 min. Add onion and parsley and cook until onions are transparent. Add seasonings and flour. Stir until smooth. Gradually add broth and sherry, stirring constantly. Cook, stirring, until sauce is thickened and smooth. Yield: 2 cups.

CHEESE DILL SAUCE

        2   tbsp butter
        2   tbsp flour
        1   cup milk
    1/3   cup cream
    1/2   cup grated Cheddar cheese
        1   tsp dill weed
    1/4   tsp salt

Melt butter and stir in flour until well blended. Gradually add milk
and cream, stirring constantly. Cook, stirring over low heat until
sauce is thickened and smooth. Add cheese, dill and salt. Stir until
melted. Yield: 1¾ cups.

DILL SAUCE

        1   egg, beaten
        1   tsp salt
        1   tsp sugar
            freshly ground black pepper to taste
        4   tsp lemon juice
        1   tsp minced onion
        2   tbsp dill weed
    1½   cups sour cream

Thoroughly combine all ingredients. Refrigerate to allow flavors to
blend. Yield: 1¾ cups.

QUICK PARSLEY SAUCE

        1   can (10½-oz) cream of celery soup
    1/2   cup milk
        2   tbsp chopped parsley

Combine undiluted soup and milk and heat, stirring until very hot.
Add parsley. Yield: 1¾ cups.

ENTRÉES   97

HOLLANDAISE SAUCE

Blender

   1/2   cup butter
     3   egg yolks
     2   tbsp lemon juice
   1/4   tsp salt
         dash of cayenne pepper

Heat butter to bubbling. Do not brown. Pour egg yolks, lemon juice, salt and cayenne in blender. With motor on low speed, gradually add hot butter and blend until sauce is thickened and smooth. Yield: 3/4 cup.

FLUFFY MUSTARD SAUCE

     1   tbsp sugar
     3   tbsp prepared mustard
     2   tbsp vinegar
     1   tbsp water
   3/4   tsp salt
     2   egg yolks, slightly beaten
     1   tbsp butter, melted
   2-3   tsp horseradish
   1/2   cup heavy cream, whipped

Add sugar, prepared mustard, vinegar, water and salt to the beaten egg yolks. Cook over hot water, not boiling, and stir until thickened. Stir in butter and horseradish. Remove from heat and cool thoroughly. Fold in whipped cream. Serve at room temperature. Yield: 1¼ cups.

Salads and Dressings

For LADIES WHO LUNCH and count calories, salads are greatly enjoyed as side dishes and enthusiastically endorsed as main courses. Nothing seems more slimming than a tossed green salad. A "dab" of dressing doesn't count.

The cardinal rule in serving a salad is "the prettier it looks, the better it tastes." Every serving of salad from an elegant mousse and colorful fruit to a lettuce or tomato should be served with an artistic flair. Use carrot curls, radish flowers, cucumber strips, celery leaves, parsley sprigs or whatever else comes to hand or mind. Garnish with a painter's eye to color and form.

Molded salads are one of the most eye-catching luncheon dishes. The mysterious workings of setting gelatin will present no problem, if a few instructions are faithfully followed. Unmolding is simple with these three easy steps. (1) Loosen the mold in several places with a flat knife and rap the mold to loosen the gelatin vacuum. (2) Prepare the platter by first thoroughly chilling it and then slightly moistening the surface to center the mold more easily. (3) Reverse the mold onto the plate, cover with a hot towel and shake it lightly. Dipping the mold in warm water for a few seconds should only be a last resort. Too often the salad begins to melt away.

Fruits are especially colorful in salads. They are light but flavorsome, and the plainest berry or melon ball looks fancy when served in a basket made from an orange shell, pineapple half or watermelon rind. Sweet dressings are especially good with fruit salads. To prevent fresh fruits such as apples, fresh peaches, and pears from discoloring, combine one quart of water and the juice of half a lemon. Pour over the fruit. They may stand for several hours.

The difference between a crisp, glistening bowl of greens and a wet, limp salad is a few simple procedures. Prepare the greens in advance by washing in cold running water, draining thoroughly, tearing them into bite-sized pieces and rolling in a towel to dry. Place the greens in a plastic bag in the refrigerator to chill. The bowl and plates should also be chilled as heat wilts the leaves. Add a minimum amount of dressing to barely moisten, not to drown, the leaves and then toss gently. Dressing and any moist ingredients such as tomato should only be added at the last minute. Contrary to popular opinion, salad bowls should be washed or the oil will become rancid.

Tastes in salad dressings are highly personal. Experiment with herbs and seasonings. Plain first-quality oil and vinegar are superb but hardly adventuresome. Now is the time to forget instructions and season with intuition. A dash of an herb or a splash of a sauce can turn an ordinary green salad into a hostess's speciality fit for a four-star recommendation.

APRICOT SALAD
Blender

    1   pkg (6-oz) apricot-flavored gelatin
    2   cups boiling water
    1   can (12-oz) apricot nectar
    1   pkg (8-oz) cream cheese

Dissolve gelatin in boiling water. Place in blender with apricot nectar and cream cheese broken into chunks. Blend until smooth. Pour into a 5-cup mold which has been rinsed with cold water. Refrigerate until firm, about 3 hr. Unmold on crisp salad greens. Serves 6–8.

BING CHERRY SALAD

    2   cans (8¾-oz) pitted Bing cherries
1/2   cup water
    1   pkg (3-oz) black cherry-flavored gelatin
1/2   cup port wine

Drain cherries, reserving 1 cup of syrup. Bring syrup and water to a boil. Remove from heat. Add gelatin and stir to dissolve. Add wine and cherries. Pour into 5-cup mold which has been rinsed with cold water. Refrigerate 4–6 hr. or until firm. Unmold on lettuce leaves or water cress. Salad may be served with Mayonnaise Dressing (p. 121). Serves 6.

ENDIVE AND GRAPEFRUIT SALAD

    9   small heads endive
    3   large grapefruit
    1   small red onion, very thinly sliced

Wash and trim endive. Dry thoroughly and crisp in refrigerator until serving time. Peel and remove all white membrane from grapefruit. Divide into sections. Arrange endive on platter. Top with grapefruit sections and onion slices. May be served with Sweet French Dressing (p. 120). Serves 6.

BACON AND LETTUCE SALAD

1 qt leaf or Boston lettuce
4 scallions, sliced
4 slices bacon, crisply cooked and crumbled
1/2 cup light cream
1 tbsp sugar
1/4 tsp salt
3½ tbsp vinegar

Wash, dry and trim lettuce. It is essential to crisp salad greens in refrigerator for several hours before using. Combine remaining ingredients to make a dressing. Mix thoroughly. Toss crisp lettuce lightly with dressing. Serves 6.

COTTAGE-CHEESE MOLD WITH FRESH FRUIT

3 tbsp unflavored gelatin
1¼ cups fresh orange juice
1 cup water
6 tbsp sugar
6 tbsp fresh lemon juice
1/2 tsp salt
1½ cups creamed cottage cheese
1½ cups seedless grapes, halved
2 cups chopped mixed fresh fruit

Soften gelatin in 3/4 cup of orange juice for 5 min. Heat remaining 1/2 cup of orange juice and water and stir in softened gelatin until dissolved. Add sugar, lemon juice and salt. Press cottage cheese through a sieve and add to gelatin mixture. Mix thoroughly. Refrigerate until mixture just begins to set. Beat with a rotary beater until fluffy, about 2 min. Arrange 10 or 12 grape halves around bottom of 6-cup ring mold which has been rinsed with cold water. Fold remaining grapes into the gelatin mixture and spoon into mold. Chill until firm or about 3 hr. Unmold on salad greens and fill with fresh fruit of your choice. Serves 6.

BROCCOLI MOUSSE

1½ tbsp unflavored gelatin
1/2 cup water
1 tbsp grated onion
2 tsp lemon juice
2 tbsp Worcestershire sauce
  dash of cayenne pepper
1/2 tsp salt
1 cup mayonnaise
1 cup heavy cream, whipped
1 pkg (10-oz) broccoli flowerets, cooked
  Garnish: tomatoes

Soften gelatin in water for 5 min. Then heat it *over* hot water to dissolve. Meanwhile add onion, lemon juice, Worcestershire, cayenne and salt to mayonnaise. Fold whipped cream and gelatin into mayonnaise mixture. Fold in well-drained broccoli. Pour into 5-cup ring mold which has been rinsed with cold water. Chill until firm. Unmold on water cress. Mousse may be served with sliced ham, seafood or cold beef, garnished with sliced tomatoes. Serves 6–8.

CRANBERRY HORSERADISH MOUSSE

1½ tbsp unflavored gelatin
1/2 cup cold water
3 cups whole cranberry sauce
1½ cups sour cream
3 tbsp horseradish
1½ tbsp lemon juice
1/3 cup grated raw carrot

Soften gelatin in water for 5 min. Heat over hot water until the gelatin is dissolved. Combine remaining ingredients. Mix in gelatin. Pour into 5-cup mold which has been rinsed with cold water. Chill until set. Unmold on salad greens. May be served with Mayonnaise Dressing (p. 121). Serves 6.

BEET AND EGG SALAD

1	small head Boston lettuce, romaine, leaf lettuce and chicory
2	tomatoes, cut in wedges
5	stalks celery, cut into 5″ strips
1½	cups cooked beets, cut into strips
6	hard-boiled eggs, finely chopped
	fresh parsley, tarragon and chives to taste, chopped
1½	cup French Dressing (p. 120)

Shred salad greens into 1/3″ strips. Pile in center of salad bowl. Arrange prepared vegetables in attractive mounds around salad greens. Sprinkle with chopped herbs. To serve: bring to table and display unmixed, then toss with French Dressing. Serves 6.

CHEESE ASPIC WITH CURRY DRESSING

1	tbsp unflavored gelatin
2	tbsp water
1/2	cup light cream
2	pkg (3-oz) cream cheese, softened
1	cup grated sharp Chedder cheese
2	tsp Worcestershire sauce
1/2	tsp Tabasco sauce
1/2	cup chopped pecans
1	cup heavy cream, whipped
6	medium tomatoes, peeled
	Garnish: paprika

Soften gelatin in water for 5 min. Heat cream. Add gelatin and stir until dissolved. Combine with cream cheese and stir until smooth. Add Cheddar cheese, Worcestershire, Tabasco and nuts. Fold in whipped cream. Chill until mixture begins to set. Cut each tomato into 8 wedges without cutting all the way through, making a petal effect. Spread cheese mixture between wedges and in center. Garnish with paprika and a sprinkling of chopped nuts. Chill for 3–4 hr. Serve on salad greens. May be served with Curry Dressing (p. 118). Serves 6.

GINGER PEAR SALAD

    1   pkg (3-oz) lemon-flavored gelatin
    3/4 cup boiling water
    1¼ cups gingerale
    1½ tbsp chopped crystallized ginger
    3   small fresh pears, halved
        or 1 can (1-lb) pears
        cream cheese
        chopped walnuts
        Garnish: ripe olives

Dissolve gelatin in water. Add gingerale. Chill until beginning to set. Rinse 6 individual round molds or a 9″ x 9″ pan in cold water. Spoon enough gelatin in bottom of mold to cover. Put about 3/4 tsp. of ginger in center of each mold, or put 6 equal portions of ginger in pan. Place pear halves, cavity side down, over ginger. Spoon remaining gelatin over pears. Chill until firm. Unmold on salad greens and serve with cream cheese balls which have been rolled in chopped nuts. Garnish with ripe olives. Serves 6.

WALDORF SALAD MOLD

    1   pkg (3-oz) lemon-flavored gelatin
    1/4 tsp salt
    1   cup hot water
    1   cup cold water
    2   tsp vinegar
    1   cup diced, unpeeled red apples
    1/4 cup chopped walnuts
    3/4 cup diced celery

Dissolve gelatin and salt in hot water. Add cold water and vinegar. Chill until beginning to set. Fold in apples, walnuts and celery. Pour into six individual molds which have been rinsed in cold water. Chill for 2–3 hr. or until firm. Unmold and serve on lettuce leaves. Salad may be served with Mayonnaise Dressing (p. 121). Serves 6.

GRAPEFRUIT AND AVOCADO SALAD

    3   grapefruits
    2   large avocados
         juice of 1/2 lemon
    1   large banana
    3   tbsp mayonnaise
         chopped piñons
         lettuce shells
         paprika

Peel grapefruit, remove white membrane and section. Discard any seeds. Chill. To serve: peel and slice avocado. Sprinkle with lemon juice. Peel and cut banana into 6 pieces. Roll in mayonnaise and in chopped nuts. Place lettuce shells in individual salad plates. Put a piece of banana in the center of each and surround with grapefruit and avocado. Dip fingers in paprika and touch the edges of the lettuce leaves for color. Serve immediately. Serves 6.

GRAPEFRUIT-APPLE MOLD

    2   tbsp unflavored gelatin
  1/2   cup cold water
    1   medium grapefruit
  1/4   cup honey
  1/4   cup sugar
  1/4   tsp salt
  3/4   cup Sauterne wine
  1/3   cup fresh lemon juice
    1   cup diced, unpeeled apples

Soften gelatin in cold water. Peel grapefruit and remove sections, reserving juice. Add enough water to juice to make 2 cups. Heat to a boil. Remove from heat and add gelatin, stirring until dissolved. Stir in honey, sugar, salt, Sauterne and lemon juice. Chill until mixture begins to set. Fold in grapefruit sections and apples. Pour into 6-cup mold which has been rinsed with cold water. Chill until firm. To serve: unmold on salad greens. May be served with Sweet French Dressing (p. 120). Serves 6–8.

CANTALOUPE AND CUCUMBER SALAD

    2   cantaloupes, halved, peeled and seeded
        French Dressing to cover (p. 120)
    1   large cucumber, peeled and sliced
        salt
1/2   cup sour cream
    3   hard-boiled eggs, sliced

Dice cantaloupe meat and marinate in enough French Dressing to cover for at least 1 hr. Sprinkle the cucumber with salt and allow to stand for 1 hr. Drain the cantaloupe and cucumber very well and mix with sour cream. Chill for at least 1 hr. Arrange on lettuce and top with hard-boiled egg slices. Serves 8.

MELON-ORANGE MOLD

    1   tbsp unflavored gelatin
1/2   cup cold water
1/2   cup boiling water
1/3   cup sugar
1/8   tsp salt
2/3   cup orange juice
1/4   cup lemon juice
    6   very thin orange slices
    2   cups assorted small melon balls
        Garnish: fresh mint

Soften gelatin in cold water for 5 min. Add boiling water, sugar and salt. Stir until sugar and gelatin are dissolved. Add juices. Arrange orange slices in bottom of 5-cup mold which has been rinsed in cold water. Cover with a thin layer of the gelatin mixture. Chill until set or about 30 min. Refrigerate remaining gelatin until it just begins to set. Fold melon balls into gelatin mixture and pour over orange slices. Chill until firm or about 3 hr. Unmold on salad greens. Garnish with fresh mint. May be served with Mayonnaise Dressing (p. 121). Serves 6.

AVOCADO SALAD

2	avocados
2½	cups canned bean sprouts, drained
1	pimiento, cut into strips
1/4	cup chopped celery
1/2	cup sliced black olives
1/4	cup finely chopped chives
1	tbsp lime juice
1/2	cup French Dressing (P. 120)
	water cress
	Garnish: avocado

Peel and slice avocados. Mix together avocado slices, bean sprouts, pimiento, celery, olives, chives and lime juice. Add French Dressing and toss lightly to coat. Refrigerate for about 2 hr. This salad should be used within 4 hr. of preparation to prevent discoloration of the avocado. Serve on water cress and garnish with avocado slices. Serves 6.

ORANGE CHEESE SALAD BOWL

3/4	cup salad oil
2	tbsp fresh lemon juice
2	tbsp dry sherry
2½	tsp ginger
2	tsp wine vinegar
1/2	tsp salt
	dash of pepper
1/4	tsp sugar
6	cups assorted salad greens
2	pkg (3-oz) cream cheese
6	tsp grated orange peel
1½	cups seedless green grapes, halved
2	tbsp chopped green onion
1/2	cup slivered almonds, toasted

Thoroughly combine oil, lemon juice, sherry, ginger, vinegar, salt, pepper and sugar to make a dressing. Wash and tear salad greens into bite-sized pieces. Arrange in salad bowl. Press all sides of cream cheese blocks into orange peel, so that it adheres. Cut cheese into small cubes and add to greens with grapes, onions and almonds. Chill. Toss salad with dressing. This is a pretty salad to bring to the table before tossing. Serves 6.

CALIFORNIA SALAD

1	large cucumber
1/2	tsp salt
2/3	cup olive oil
1/3	cup wine vinegar
1½	tsp basil
1	tsp salt
1/2	tsp freshly ground black pepper
1/4	tsp garlic powder
8	medium-sized mushroom caps, thinly sliced
5	scallions, thinly sliced
1/2	cup minced parsley
2	large tomatoes, cut into wedges
1/2	green pepper, seeded and thinly sliced
1/2	lb Swiss cheese, cut into thin strips
3	hard-boiled eggs, sliced
	Garnish: water cress

Peel and slice the cucumber. Sprinkle with salt and allow to stand for 30 min. Combine olive oil, vinegar, basil, salt, pepper and garlic powder in the bottom of a salad bowl. Add mushrooms, scallions and drained cucumbers. Top with parsley and mix gently. Add a layer of tomatoes and green pepper. Cover the salad and refrigerate for 4 hr. To serve: top with Swiss cheese, eggs and surround with water cress. Serves 6.

FRESH TOMATO AND RICE SALAD

    6   fresh tomatoes
    2   cups cooked rice
1½   cups cooked small green peas
1/2   tsp salt
        freshly ground pepper to taste
1/4   tsp dry mustard
1/4   cup tarragon vinegar
3/4   cup salad oil

Remove skin from tomatoes. Cut a slice from top of each tomato and carefully remove pulp. Combine cooked rice and peas. Chill. Make a dressing by mixing together salt, pepper, mustard, vinegar and oil. Gently toss chilled rice and peas with just enough dressing to bind them together. Put 1 tbsp. of dressing in each tomato shell. Chill. To serve: pour out half of the dressing from each tomato and fill with rice and pea mixture. Serve on crisp salad greens. Serves 6.

PEACH-RASPBERRY SALAD

PEACH LAYER

1½   cups water
    1   pkg (3-oz) lemon-flavored gelatin
    2   tbsp lemon juice
    3   medium peaches, peeled and sliced
    2   tsp milk
    2   tbsp mayonnaise
    1   pkg (3-oz) cream cheese, softened
    2   tbsp chopped pecans

RASPBERRY LAYER

    1   pkg (10-oz) frozen raspberries, thawed
1½   cups boiling water
    2   tbsp lemon juice
    1   pkg (3-oz) raspberry-flavored gelatin

PEACH LAYER: bring 3/4 cup of the water to a boil. Add gelatin and stir until dissolved. Add lemon juice and remaining 3/4 cup water to gelatin mixture. Arrange 8 peach slices on bottom of 6-cup mold which has been rinsed in cold water. Pour gelatin mixture just to cover. Chill until almost set. Combine remaining peaches with remaining gelatin. Pour into mold and chill until set. Combine milk, mayonnaise, cream cheese and nuts. Blend thoroughly. Spread evenly on set peach layer and chill.

RASPBERRY LAYER: drain thawed raspberries very well. Reserve syrup and add 3/4 cup water. Bring remaining 3/4 cup water to a boil. Add gelatin and stir until gelatin is dissolved. Combine raspberries, raspberry syrup, gelatin mixture, and lemon juice. Pour into mold. Chill for 4–6 hr. or until firm. Unmold on salad greens. May be served with Mayonnaise Dressing (p. 121). Serves 8.

FROSTED MELON SURPRISE

1	pkg (3-oz) wild cherry-flavored gelatin
1	cup boiling water
3/4	cup cold water
1	cup fresh fruit, cut up
1	medium cantaloupe
1	pkg (8-oz) cream cheese, softened
1–2	tbsp milk

Dissolve gelatin in boiling water. Add cold water and chill until almost set. Fold fruit into thickened gelatin. Meanwhile peel melon, cut a slice from the top and scoop out the seeds. Drain well. Spoon fruit mixture into melon. There will be some left over. Replace the slice with toothpicks. Chill at least 3 hr. or until gelatin is set. Combine cream cheese and milk and beat until fluffy. Cut a thin slice from one side of the melon so that it will sit firmly on plate. Spread cheese over melon as if icing a cake. Refrigerate. To serve: remove toothpicks, slice and serve on salad greens. May be garnished with additional fresh fruit. Serves 6.

ORANGE-AND-ONION SALAD

4	navel oranges
2	heads Boston or leaf lettuce
2	red onions, thinly sliced
1/2	cup ripe olives, sliced
1/4	cup pimiento, cut in strips

Peel oranges, removing all membrane. Cut into thin slices. Wash, trim and crisp lettuce. Arrange lettuce on platter. Top with oranges, onions, olives and pimientos in that order. Chill. May be served with Sweet French Dressing (p. 120). Serves 6.

GAZPACHO SALAD MOLD

2	cans (13-oz) consommé madrilene
1/2	tsp basil
1/2	tsp thyme
2	tbsp unflavored gelatin
1/2	cup tomato juice
1/2	cup minced green onions
1/2	tsp salt
	freshly ground black pepper to taste
4	drops Tabasco sauce
2	tbsp lemon juice
1½	cups diced cucumber
1/4	cup diced green pepper
1/4	cup diced water chestnuts
	Garnish: water cress, cucumber, lemon

Heat consommé with basil and thyme. Soften gelatin in tomato juice. Add to consommé mixture. Add onions and season with salt, pepper, Tabasco sauce, and lemon juice. Chill until beginning to set. Fold in cucumber, green pepper and water chestnuts. Pour into a 6-cup ring mold which has been rinsed with cold water. Chill for 3 hr. or until firm. To serve: unmold on water cress and garnish with cucumber and lemon slices. May be served with Cheese Olive Dressing (p. 118). Serves 6–8.

SPINACH SALAD

1/2	lb washed spinach, trimmed
1	small head Boston lettuce
2½	tbsp lemon juice
1/2	cup sliced mushroom caps
	salt and freshly ground pepper to taste
1	clove garlic
6	tbsp olive oil
1/3	cup sliced water chestnuts
1/4	cup sliced green onions
2	hard-boiled eggs, sliced
1/2	lb bacon, crisply cooked and crumbled

Tear spinach and lettuce into bite-sized pieces. Chill to crisp. Sprinkle 1/2 tbsp. lemon juice over mushrooms to prevent discoloration. Prepare dressing by sprinkling bottom of salad bowl with salt and pepper and rub with garlic. Add remaining 2 tbsp. lemon juice and olive oil. Chill the bowl. To serve: add spinach, lettuce, vegetables, egg and bacon bits to bowl and toss gently to coat leaves. Serves 6.

SHRIMP-CHICK PEA SALAD

1	can (1¼ lb) chick peas, drained
1½	cups cooked shrimp, cut in large pieces
1/3	cup mayonnaise
1/3	cup chopped parsley
4	green onions, chopped
2	tbsp lemon juice
	salt to taste
1/2	tsp curry powder

Mix the chick peas with the shrimp. Combine remaining ingredients to make a dressing. Toss with the shrimp mixture and refrigerate at least 2 hr. to chill. Serve on a bed of crisp salad greens. Serves 6.

MOLDED TOMATO SALAD

2   tbsp unflavored gelatin
1/2 cup water
1   can (10 3/4-oz) tomato soup
3   pkg (3-oz) cream cheese, softened
1/2 cup chopped celery
1/2 cup chopped pimiento olives
1/3 cup chopped sweet onion
1/2 tsp celery seed
1/4 tsp cayenne pepper
1   cup mayonnaise
    Garnish: cucumber and hard-boiled egg

Soften gelatin in water for 5 min. Heat soup. Add gelatin and stir until dissolved. Place cream cheese in a bowl. Pour gelatin mixture over cheese and beat until well blended and smooth. Add vegetables, celery seed, cayenne pepper and mayonnaise. Pour into a 5-cup mold which has been rinsed in cold water. Chill at least 3 hr. or until firm. Unmold on salad greens and garnish with slices of cucumber and hard-boiled eggs. Serves 6–8.

FRESH VEGETABLE-SOUR CREAM MOLD

2   envelopes instant beef broth mix (or 2 bouillon cubes)
1   pkg (3-oz) lemon-flavored gelatin
1   cup boiling water
2   tbsp tarragon vinegar
1/2 tsp salt
1   cup sour cream
1/2 cup unpared, chopped cucumber
3   tbsp chopped green pepper
1/4 cup sliced radishes
3   tbsp sliced green onions

Dissolve instant beef broth mix or bouillon cubes and gelatin in boiling water. Add vinegar and salt and chill until gelatin just begins to set. Fold in sour cream and add vegetables. Pour into

4-cup mold which has been rinsed in cold water. Chill for about 4 hr. or until firm. Unmold on salad greens and garnish with a few slices of cucumber and radish. Serves 6.

STRAWBERRY SOUR CREAM MOLD

1	pkg (3-oz) strawberry-flavored gelatin
3/4	cup boiling water
1	pkg (10-oz) frozen strawberries, thawed
1	can (8½-oz) crushed pineapple, drained
2	medium bananas, sliced
1½	cups sour cream

Dissolve gelatin in water. Add strawberries, pineapple and bananas. Pour half of this mixture into a 6-cup mold which has been rinsed with cold water. Chill until set. Spread sour cream over set layer. Chill for at least 1 hr. Pour remaining mixture on top. Chill until set, about 2 hr. Unmold on salad greens. Serves 6.

SHRIMP AND AVOCADO SALAD

1½	lbs small cooked shrimp
3/4	cup finely chopped celery
3	tbsp lemon juice
3	tbsp pineapple juice
1/2	tsp salt
1/4	tsp pepper
1/2	tsp curry powder
2	medium avocados

Combine the shrimp with the celery and chill. Mix the lemon juice, pineapple juice, salt, pepper, and curry powder together to make a dressing. Chill. To serve: halve and pit the avocado and scoop out avocado balls, using a melon ball cutter. Mix with the shrimp mixture and toss lightly with the dressing. Serve on crisp salad greens. Serves 6.

RASPBERRY RING

1	pkg (10-oz) frozen raspberries, thawed
1	tbsp unflavored gelatin
1/4	cup lemon juice
1/2	cup water
1/4	cup sugar
1/4	tsp salt
1/4	cup cantaloupe balls

Drain raspberries, reserving syrup. Soften gelatin in lemon juice for 5 min. Add water to reserved syrup to make 1 cup of liquid. Bring to boil and add gelatin. Stir until dissolved. Stir in sugar, salt and raspberries. Chill until mixture begins to set. Arrange melon balls in the bottom of a 5-cup ring mold which has been rinsed with cold water. Pour gelatin mixture over melon. Chill until set. Unmold on salad greens. May be served filled with chicken salad and accompanied by Mayonnaise Dressing (p. 121). Serves 6.

WESTERN SALAD

1/2	clove garlic
2	tbsp salad oil
3	qt salad greens
1/3	cup salad oil
1/3	cup freshly grated Parmesan cheese
1/3	cup crumbled blue cheese
	salt and pepper to taste
1	egg, beaten
	juice of 2 lemons
2	cups croutons

Soak garlic in oil for at least 1 hr. Prepare greens by washing, drying and crisping them in refrigerator. To serve: tear greens into bite-sized pieces. Add 1/3 cup oil, Parmesan, blue cheese, salt and pepper. Break egg onto greens and sprinkle lemon juice over the salad. Toss well. Remove garlic from oil. Combine garlic flavored oil with croutons and sprinkle over top. Serves 8.

GARDEN VEGETABLE MOLD

2	tbsp unflavored gelatin
2½	cups water
4	tsp sugar
1	tsp salt
3/4	cup lemon juice
1	cup finely chopped celery
1	cup finely chopped radishes
1/2	cup finely chopped green pepper
1/2	cup finely chopped cauliflower
1/2	cup finely chopped cucumber

Soften gelatin in 1/2 cup water for 5 min. Heat remaining water, sugar, salt and lemon juice. Add gelatin and stir until dissolved. Chill until mixture just begins to set. Add chopped vegetables. Turn into a 5-cup ring mold or 6 individual molds which have been rinsed with cold water. Chill about 4 hr. or until firm. Unmold on crisp salad greens. This may be served with Mayonnaise Dressing (p. 121). Serves 6.

SWEET AND SOUR LETTUCE

3	qt Boston or leaf lettuce
3	tbsp chopped chives or sweet onion
3	slices of bacon
1/3	cup vinegar
2	tsp sugar
	salt and pepper to taste

Tear lettuce into bite-sized pieces and add onion. Fry bacon until crisp and drain thoroughly. Add vinegar, sugar, salt and pepper to pan drippings. Mix well. Pour hot vinegar mixture over lettuce and toss lightly. Garnish with crumbled bacon and serve immediately. Serves 6–8.

CHEESE-OLIVE DRESSING

　　　2　pkg (3-oz) cream cheese, softened
　　1/4　cup mayonnaise
　　1/2　cup light cream
　　1/2　cup chopped ripe olives
　　　1　tsp Worcestershire sauce
　　　　dash of Tabasco sauce

Cream the cheese with mayonnaise and cream until smooth. Add remaining ingredients. Mix well. Dressing may be served with molded vegetable salads. Yield: 1⅓ cups.

CUCUMBER SOUR CREAM DRESSING
Blender

　　3/4　cup sour cream
　　1/4　cup mayonnaise
　　　1　small cucumber, peeled and cut up
　　3/4　tsp salt
　　1½　tsp dill weed
　　　2　tbsp grated onion

Combine ingredients in blender and blend until smooth. Dressing may be served with tossed or tomato salad. Yield: 1½ cups.

CURRY DRESSING
Blender

　　1½　tsp salt
　　　2　tsp curry powder
　　1/2　tsp pepper
　　3/4　cup olive oil
　　1/2　cup vinegar

Place all ingredients in a blender and blend for about 10 sec. Dressing may be served on fruit or green salad. Yield: 1¼ cups.

SPICE DRESSING
Blender

1/3	cup	fresh lemon juice
		rind of two lemons, grated
3/4	cup	olive oil
		dash of Tabasco sauce
1/2	tsp	garlic powder
1/2	tsp	coriander
1/2	tsp	cumin seed
1/2	tsp	dry mustard
1½	tsp	sugar
1/2	tsp	paprika

Combine all the ingredients and blend until smooth. This dressing is good with fruit or tomato salads. Yield: 1 cup.

RUBY SALAD DRESSING
Blender

1/2	cup	currant jelly
4	tbsp	salad oil
2	tbsp	lemon juice
		dash of onion juice

Place ingredients in blender and blend until smooth. Dressing may be served on fruit salad. Yield 3/4 cup.

RUSSIAN DRESSING

1	cup	mayonnaise
1/3	cup	chili sauce
1	tbsp	lemon juice
1	tsp	Worcestershire sauce

Thoroughly combine all ingredients and chill. Yield: 1⅓ cups.

CURRY MAYONNAISE

    1   cup mayonnaise
    2   tsp cream
  1/2   tsp ginger
    2   tsp curry powder
  1/4   tsp garlic powder
    3   tsp honey
    1   tbsp lemon juice

Combine all the ingredients, mixing well. Goes well with fruit, fish or chicken salads. When serving with shrimp or chicken salads, 1 tbsp. chopped chutney and 1 tbsp. toasted slivered almonds may be added. Yield: 1 cup.

FRENCH DRESSING

    1   cup olive oil
  1/4   cup vinegar
        juice of 1 lemon
    1   tsp salt
    1   tbsp sugar
  1/2   tsp Worcestershire sauce
  1/2   tsp paprika
  1/4   tsp garlic powder
        freshly ground black pepper to taste

Combine all ingredients in a jar with a tight-fitting lid. Shake well. Refrigerate. Yield: 1¼ cups.

SWEET FRENCH DRESSING

    1   cup sugar
    1   onion, grated
    1   cup vinegar
    1   cup salad oil

1 tsp salt
2 tsp paprika
2 tsp celery seed

Put sugar and onion in a 1-qt. jar with a tight lid. Allow to stand for at least 1 hr. Add other ingredients and shake until very well blended. Yield: 3 cups.

FRENCH-MAYONNAISE DRESSING

1 cup mayonnaise
1 cup French Dressing
1/4 tsp garlic powder
1 tsp anchovy fillet, mashed
1/2 cup freshly grated Parmesan cheese

Combine all the ingredients, mixing well. May be served on tossed green salads. Yield: 2½ cups.

MAYONNAISE DRESSING

1/4 cup heavy cream
     or
1/2 cup sour cream
1 cup mayonnaise
2 tsp vinegar
3 tsp sugar
1-2 tbsp milk

Whip the heavy cream. Fold whipped cream (or sour cream) into the mayonnaise and flavor with vinegar and sugar. Add enough milk for desired consistency. Dressing may be used on fruit or chicken salad. Yield: 2 cups.

GREEN DRESSING
Blender

        2   tbsp vinegar
        6   tbsp olive oil
        3   tbsp prepared sharp mustard
    1/2   tsp garlic salt
        6   anchovy fillets, mashed
    1/2   tsp salt
        1   tbsp finely chopped parsley
        1   tbsp finely chopped chives
        1   hard-boiled egg

Combine all ingredients in blender and blend until smooth. Dressing goes well with shellfish. Yield: 3/4 cup.

TARRAGON SALAD DRESSING
Blender

        1   clove garlic
        4   scallions, chopped
        1   tbsp tarragon
            juice of 1 lemon
    1/2   tsp dry mustard
        2   egg yolks
    1/3   cup red wine vinegar
    1/2   tsp Tabasco sauce
            salt and pepper to taste
    1½   cups olive oil

Put all ingredients except olive oil in the blender. Blend for 10 sec. and then gradually add olive oil while blending. Dressing may be served on salad greens, fruit or chicken salad. Yield: 2 cups.

WESTERN DRESSING

    1/2   tsp dry mustard
        1   tbsp hot water

1/2	cup sugar
2	tsp salt
1/2	tsp paprika
1	clove of garlic, cut
1/2	cup ketchup
1/3	cup vinegar
1/2	tsp Worcestershire sauce
1	cup olive oil
1	small onion, grated

Moisten mustard with hot water. Add the remaining ingredients and shake well in a tightly covered jar. Shake before each serving. Yield: 2¼ cups.

HORSERADISH DRESSING

1/4	cup grated horseradish
1	cup sour cream
2	tbsp mayonnaise
1	tsp sugar
1/4	tsp salt
1	tsp dill weed

Combine ingredients and refrigerate for at least 1 hr. Dressing is good served with molded vegetable salads. Yield: 1¼ cups.

LIME-HONEY DRESSING

1/3	cup frozen undiluted limeade, thawed
1/3	cup honey
1/3	cup salad oil
1	tsp celery seed

Combine all the ingredients and mix well. Dressing is good served on a tart fruit salad. Yield: 1 cup.

SOUR CREAM DRESSING

1	egg, beaten
2–3	tbsp sugar
1	tbsp flour
1¼	tsp salt
1/4	tsp dry mustard
1/4	cup wine vinegar
1	cup milk
1/2	cup sour cream

Combine egg and dry ingredients in a saucepan. Slowly stir in vinegar and milk. Cook over low heat, stirring constantly, until dressing is slightly thickened. Cool. Stir in sour cream. This dressing is best served on shredded cabbage or lettuce. Yield: 1½ cups.

TANGY CHEESE DRESSING

1	cup mayonnaise
1/3	cup commercial creamy French dressing
1½	tsp anchovy paste
1	crushed garlic clove
1/3	cup freshly grated Parmesan cheese
	Garnish: garlic croutons

Combine ingredients and mix well. This dressing may be served with green salads and croutons as a garnish. Yield: 1⅔ cups.

WINE DRESSING

1/2	cup fresh lemon juice
1/4	tsp salt
1/2	cup sugar
1/4	cup dry sherry

Combine ingredients in a jar. Shake very well before serving. Yield: 3/4 cup.

SALAD IDEAS

VEGETABLE SALADS

1. Sliced green pepper, onion, water chestnuts, celery and mushrooms combined with spinach and Boston lettuce. Good with an oil and vinegar dressing.
2. Cottage cheese with slices of tomato, cucumber, onion and diced green pepper served on lettuce shells. Try it with Cucumber Sour Cream Dressing (p. 118).
3. Small tomatoes stuffed with a mixture of cottage cheese, minced chives and toasted slivered almonds served on greens accompanied by Mayonnaise Dressing (p. 121); or stuffed with grated cabbage combined with Sour Cream Dressing (p. 124), and served on greens garnished with fresh mint leaves.
4. Grated raw carrot, diced celery, raisins and nuts served on greens accompanied by Mayonnaise Dressing (p. 121).
5. Cooked asparagus tips topped with grated Cheddar cheese and sieved hard-boiled eggs on tomato slices served on greens with Sweet French Dressing (p. 120).
6. Shredded red cabbage, beets and parsnips, topped with cucumber slices and purple onion rings and served in a lettuce cup. Good with Horseradish Dressing (p. 123).
7. Cauliflower florets, sliced tomato, sprigs of fresh mint tossed with salad greens and a French dressing.
8. Sliced radishes, purple onion rings and cucumber, combined with endive and chicory, and tossed with French-Mayonnaise Dressing (p. 121).
9. Artichoke hearts, sliced tomato, purple onion rings and seived hard-boiled egg combined with greens and Western Dressing (p. 122).

FRUIT SALAD

1. Sliced fresh pears or peaches, green grapes and chopped nuts served on greens accompanied by Ruby Salad Dressing (p. 119).
2. Pitted Bing cherries served in the hollow of a halved fresh peach on a lettuce leaf. Good with Mayonnaise Dressing (p. 121).
3. Banana slices, spread with mayonnaise and rolled in finely chopped peanuts, served on greens with Lime-Honey Dressing (p. 123).
4. Orange slices and carrot curls served on lettuce, water cress or spinach. Try it with Curry Dressing (p. 118).
5. Fresh pear halves topped with grated Cheddar cheese served on water cress with Sweet French Dressing (p. 120).
6. Chopped, unpeeled apple, celery, green grapes and chopped walnuts combined with mayonnaise and served in lettuce shells.
7. Dried prunes or apricots stuffed with cream cheese, cottage cheese or peanut butter served on greens.
8. Avocado, fresh pineapple and melon slices served on greens. Good with Wine Dressing (p. 124).
9. Fresh pineapple spears, strawberries and minced fresh mint served on Boston lettuce accompanied by Ruby Dressing (p. 119).
10. Avocado, orange and grapefruit slices, purple onion rings served on water cress with Sweet French Dressing (p. 120).
11. Melon balls, green grapes and pitted Bing cherries combined with salad greens and tossed with Tarragon Dressing (p. 122).
12. Fresh or canned pineapple spears topped with cottage cheese and slivered toasted almonds served on Boston lettuce with Mayonnaise Dressing (p. 121).

Desserts

For those with a sweet tooth, dessert is without question the *pièce de résistance*. It is the climax of every well-planned menu and hopefully makes a dramatic entrance accompanied by the guests' sighs of mouthwatering anticipation. This is the last course served and completes the picture of delicious food and warm hospitality. Any self-respecting cook feels compelled to produce something special for dessert.

Although ice cream has been a beloved standby since Marco Polo brought it west from China, its appearance at the end of the meal is unlikely to bring forth appreciative raves from your guests. Every cook desires the show-stopping effect of golden meringues, high, fluffy soufflés, or shimmering chiffons.

These desert recipes for LADIES WHO LUNCH are all spectacular to serve but are especially easy to prepare. A wide variety is included to please everyone; the pie fancier, the chocolate eater, and the "I'm-on-a-diet, I-hope-you're-serving-fruit" guest. Even everyday-sounding fare such as custard or fruit can be prepared with fancy sauces and unusual garnishes to produce an elegant dish with an intriguing taste.

Always select your dessert to complement the entrée. If the main dish is rich and filling, the dessert should be light and airy; or if the entrée is salad or soup, the course to follow can be very, very sweet. The last bite should leave the guests wanting "just a wee bit more." Don't give it to them. This is a great tribute to the cook. Don't spoil it by indulging their instinct to eat too much of a good thing.

Most of the recipes can be made ahead and the garnishes put on at the last minute. Many may be frozen. Always wrap the dish securely in foil and then place in a plastic bag and seal for freezer storage.

LAYERED APRICOT BARS

CRUST

1/2	cup butter, softened
1/4	cup sugar
1	cup sifted flour

FILLING

1/3	cup flour
1/2	tsp baking powder
1/4	tsp salt
3/4	cup light brown sugar, packed
2	eggs, beaten
3/4	cup dried apricots
1/2	cup chopped walnuts
1	tsp vanilla
	confectioners' sugar

Preheat oven to 350°.

CRUST: mix butter, sugar and flour until crumbly. Pat into greased 8" square pan. Bake for about 20 min.

FILLING: sift together flour, baking powder and salt. Gradually beat brown sugar into eggs. Add flour mixture. Mix thoroughly. Cover the apricots with water and boil about 10 min., or until tender. Drain and chop. Add the apricots, nuts and vanilla to the filling. Spread over baked crust. Bake 30 min. Cool and cut into bars. Sift confectioners' sugar over the bars. Yield: 24 bars.

APRICOT CHIFFON PIE

1	tbsp unflavored gelatin
1½	tbsp fresh lemon juice
2	eggs, separated
1	can (12-oz) apricot nectar
1/4	tsp salt
1/2	cup sugar
1/2	cup heavy cream, whipped
1	9" baked pie shell
	Garnish: dried apricots and mint leaves

Soften gelatin in lemon juice for 5 min. Beat egg yolks slightly and add apricot nectar, salt and 1/4 cup of sugar. Cook over very low heat, stirring constantly, until slightly thickened. Remove from heat. Add gelatin to hot mixture, stirring, until dissolved. Chill until mixture is just beginning to set. Beat egg whites until stiff, adding gradually the remaining 1/4 cup sugar. Fold into apricot mixture. Fold in whipped cream. Pile into baked pie shell. Chill until firm. Serve garnished with slivers of dried apricot and mint leaves. Serves 6–8.

APRICOT PARFAIT

    1   can (1-lb) pitted apricots
    2   tbsp sugar
1/4   lb peanut brittle
1/2   tsp vanilla
    1   cup heavy cream, whipped
        Garnish: whipped cream and peanut brittle

Drain syrup from apricots into a saucepan. Stir in sugar and cook until syrup is reduced and thick, about 8 min. Cool quickly in refrigerator or freezer. Purée apricots in blender. Using a rolling pin, crush peanut brittle between sheets of wax paper. Combine syrup, apricots, peanut brittle and vanilla. Fold in whipped cream and spoon into individual sherbet glasses. Refrigerate for at least 2 hr. Serve topped with a dollop of whipped cream and a few bits of peanut brittle. Serves 6.

TOASTED ALMOND-ORANGE MOUSSE

    1   tbsp unflavored gelatin
3/4   cup cold water
    1   cup sugar
    3   tbsp grated orange rind
    1   cup orange juice
1/4   cup lemon juice
3/4   cup heavy cream, whipped
    1   cup slivered almonds, toasted

Soak gelatin in 1/4 cup cold water for 5 min. Combine the sugar, grated orange rind and remaining 1/2 cup water, and bring to boil. Simmer, stirring occasionally, until syrup is formed or about 1 min. Stir gelatin into hot syrup to dissolve. Add orange and lemon juice. Chill until gelatin begins to thicken or about 2 hr. Fold orange mixture into whipped cream and add almonds. Pile in sherbet dishes and return to refrigerator until ready to serve. Serve each garnished with a small piece of almond. Serves 8.

AMBROSIA

    3   cups fresh or frozen pineapple chunks
    5   medium oranges, peeled and sectioned
    2   cups green seedless grapes
  1/2   cup orange juice
    1   can (3½-oz) shredded coconut
    2   bananas, sliced
    1   cup maraschino cherries
    1   cup gingerale

Arrange the pineapple, oranges, and grapes artistically in a crystal bowl. Sprinkle with coconut. Cover and chill. To serve: add the bananas and cherries to the fruit and pour the gingerale over all. Serve immediately. Serves 6-8.

BUTTERSCOTCH CHEWS

  1/2   cup butter, softened
    1   cup light brown sugar, packed
    1   tsp vanilla
    1   egg
  3/4   cup sifted flour
    1   tsp baking powder
    1   tsp salt
  1/2   cup chopped walnuts

Preheat oven to 400°.
Cream butter with sugar. Add vanilla and egg, beating until fluffy. Sift dry ingredients together and thoroughly combine with sugar mixture. Stir in nuts. Drop by scant teaspoons 3"–4" apart on a greased cookie sheet. Bake for 5 min. Cool for just 2 min. and then carefully remove each cookie by pressing the sharp edge of a spatula under the cookie and quickly scraping it off the sheet. Yield: 4 dozen cookies.

CHILLED CANTALOUPE AND BLUEBERRIES

3	small cantaloupes
1/2	cup Kirsch
4	tbsp confectioners' sugar
3	tsp lime juice
1½	pts blueberries

Cut melons in half and scoop out seeds. Combine remaining ingredients and spoon into center of each melon half. Refrigerate for at least 1 hr. before serving. Serves 6.

CHEESECAKE

CRUST

1⅔	cups crushed vanilla wafers
1/4	cup sugar
1/4	lb butter, softened

FILLING

1	cup sugar
1	lb cream cheese, softened
5	eggs, separated
1	pt sour cream
1	tsp vanilla
1	tsp lemon juice
2	tsp grated lemon rind

Preheat oven to 275°.

CRUST: combine vanilla wafer crumbs, sugar and softened butter. Press into bottom of a 9" spring form pan.

FILLING: cream sugar with cream cheese until fluffy. Beat egg yolks. Thoroughly combine the cheese mixture, egg yolks, sour cream, vanilla, lemon juice and lemon rind. Beat egg whites until stiff. Fold into cheese mixture. Pour mixture into prepared crust. Bake for 1 hr. Turn off heat. Allow to remain in oven with door closed for 1 hr. Open door and leave in oven for an additional hour. Place cheesecake under broiler until lightly browned. Refrigerate overnight before serving. Serves 8–10.

FROZEN CHERRY JUBILEE PIE

CRUST

1/2	cup saltine cracker crumbs
2/3	cup sugar
1/3	cup chopped pecans
2	egg whites
1/2	tsp vanilla

FILLING

1	pt vanilla ice cream, softened

TOPPING

1	can (1-lb) pitted Bing cherries
1	tbsp cornstarch
1	tbsp sugar
1/8	tsp salt
1/4	cup light corn syrup
1	tsp brandy
3/4	tsp butter

Preheat oven to 350°.
CRUST: combine cracker crumbs, 1/3 cup sugar and pecans. Beat egg whites until stiff, gradually adding the remaining 1/3 cup sugar and vanilla. Fold cracker mixture into egg whites. Spoon into a greased and floured 9" pie plate and spread to form a shell. Bake for 25 min. Cool thoroughly. It does not remain puffed. Fill center with softened ice cream and freeze for 1 hr.
TOPPING: drain cherries, reserving 1/2 cup of the syrup. Combine cherry syrup with cornstarch, sugar, salt and corn syrup. Cook, stirring until sauce is thickened and smooth. Simmer for 2 min., stirring constantly. Remove from heat. Add cherries, brandy and butter. Cool *thoroughly*. Spread over frozen ice cream. Wrap securely in foil and freeze. Serves 6–8.

CHOCOLATE BAVARIAN CREAM
Blender

       2   tbsp unflavored gelatin
     1/4   cup cold water
     1/2   cup boiling water
       1   pkg (6-oz) semisweet chocolate pieces
       1   tbsp sugar
       2   egg yolks
       1   cup light cream
       1   heaping cup crushed ice
           Garnish: chocolate curls

Soften gelatin in 1/4 cup cold water for 5 min. Pour in blender and blend with 1/2 cup boiling water. Add chocolate and sugar. Blend until smooth. Leaving the motor on, add egg yolks, cream and crushed ice. Blend until mixture just begins to thicken. Pour into 4-cup dessert mold or special serving bowl and garnish with chocolate curls. Refrigerate for at least 2 hr. Serves 6.

CHOCOLATE CUPS À LA MODE

CHOCOLATE CUP

       6   ounces semi-sweet chocolate
       2   tbsp butter

FILLING

       6   rounds of sponge cake
     1/4   cup Grand Marnier
       1   cup vanilla ice cream
       1   cup sliced fresh strawberries
     1/4   cup heavy cream
       2   tbsp sugar
           Garnish: whole strawberries

CHOCOLATE CUP: melt chocolate and butter together and stir until smooth. Swirl melted chocolate around the bottom and sides of

6 paper muffin cups, covering the entire surface. Place chocolate cups in muffin pans and chill. Peel off paper and refrigerate until ready to use.

FILLING: place a round of sponge cake to fit bottom of each chocolate cup. Sprinkle each sponge cake round with 1 tsp. Grand Marnier. Cover with a small scoop of ice cream and a handful of berries. Sprinkle 1 tsp. Grand Marnier on each. Whip cream with sugar and garnish the cups with a dollop of whipped cream and a small whole strawberry. Serves 6.

BANANES FLAMBÉES

- 6 bananas
- 4 tbsp butter, melted
- 3 tbsp light brown sugar
- 1 tsp cinnamon
- 2 jiggers of rum

Split bananas lengthwise and place in skillet with melted butter. Mix the sugar and cinnamon and sprinkle half the mixture on the bananas and sauté until light brown. Turn and sprinkle with remaining sugar mixture. To serve: add rum and ignite. Serve immediately. Be sure each plate gets its share of sauce! Bananas may be cooked at the table in a chafing dish. Serves 6.

STEWED RHUBARB AND STRAWBERRIES

- 2 lbs rhubarb
- 2 tbsp water
- 2/3–1 cup sugar
- 1 lb frozen strawberry halves, thawed

Wash, trim and cut rhubarb into 1" pieces. Place rhubarb, water and sugar in saucepan. Cover and simmer until rhubarb is tender or about 15 min. Drain excess liquid. Add strawberries and chill. Serves 6–8.

BROWN SUGAR CUSTARD

    3   cups heavy cream
    6   tbsp sugar
    6   egg yolks, beaten
    2   tsp vanilla
  1/2   cup light brown sugar, packed

Preheat oven to 300°.
Heat cream over very low heat or hot water and stir in sugar until
dissolved. Pour hot cream mixture into egg yolks, stirring constantly. Add vanilla. Pour into a 1-qt. baking dish and place dish
in a pan containing 1″ of hot water. Bake for about 45 min. or until
a knife inserted into the custard comes out clean. Chill for at least
3 hr. An hour or 2 before serving, sprinkle brown sugar on custard.
Place under broiler until sugar is melted. Refrigerate until serving
time. Serves 6–8.

CRISPY CHOCOLATE COOKIES

    1   cup sifted cake flour
    1   cup sifted confectioners' sugar
  2½   tbsp cocoa
  1/4   tsp salt
  1/2   cup butter, softened
    1   tsp vanilla

Preheat oven to 300°.
Sift flour, sugar, cocoa and salt together. Cream butter with vanilla
until fluffy. Gradually add dry ingredients to butter, beating constantly until smooth. Drop dough by very scant teaspoons on a
cookie sheet 3″–4″ apart. Flatten each with tines of a fork, form-
ing a crisscross pattern. Bake for 12 min. Cool for 1 min. Remove
cookies to waxpaper. Sift confectioners' sugar over them. Yield:
36 cookies.

CHOCOLATE POT DE CRÈME

        2   cups heavy cream
     1/4   cup sugar
        8   ounces sweet chocolate
            or 5 ounces if less chocolate is desired
        6   egg yolks
        1   tsp vanilla

Heat cream and sugar over very low heat or in top of double boiler. Stir to dissolve sugar. Melt chocolate over hot water. Remove chocolate from heat and stir into cream mixture. Beat egg yolks and gradually pour into hot chocolate mixture, beating continuously. Cook, stirring constantly, until mixture thickens or about 15 min. Remove from heat and add vanilla. Pour into pot de crème dishes, demitasse cups or into small custard cups. Refrigerate for at least 3 hr. or until well chilled. Serves 6–8.

CHOCOLATE TORTE

     1/2   cup butter, softened
     3/4   cup sifted confectioners' sugar
        4   egg yolks
        4   ounces unsweetened chocolate
     1/4   cup cognac
     3/4   cup water
      24   ladyfingers

Cream butter with sugar until fluffy. Add egg yolks, one at a time, beating after each addition. Thoroughly mix in melted chocolate. Combine cognac and water in a shallow pan. Dip the ladyfingers quickly, one at a time, in the liquid and place on an oval platter in a row of eight. Frost with one-third of the chocolate mixture. Build up 2 more layers of ladyfingers, frosting each with chocolate mixture. Completely frost top and sides of loaf. Refrigerate for at least 3 hr. Serve thoroughly chilled sliced in small portions. Serves 8.

CHOCOLATE MACAROONS

3/4 cup sugar
2 tbsp cocoa
1/4 tsp salt
2 egg whites
1 tsp vanilla
1¾ cups shredded coconut

Preheat oven to 300°.
Combine sugar, cocoa and salt in a saucepan. Beat egg whites until stiff and fold into cocoa mixture. Cook, stirring constantly, for about 5 min. Remove from heat and add vanilla and coconut. Mix thoroughly. Drop by teaspoonfuls on a greased cookie sheet. Bake for 15 min. or until puffed. Cool on rack. Yield: 20 cookies.

CHOCOLATE NUT CRUNCH

2 cups crushed vanilla wafers
1 cup finely chopped pecans
1/2 cup butter, softened
1 cup sugar
3 eggs, separated
1½ ounces unsweetened chocolate, melted
1/2 tsp vanilla
Garnish: whipped cream

Combine wafer crumbs with pecans. Line a buttered 9" square pan with half of this crumb mixture. Set aside the remaining mixture. Cream butter with sugar, beating until light and fluffy. Add egg yolks, one at a time, beating well after each addition. Add chocolate and vanilla. Mix thoroughly. Beat egg whites until stiff and fold into the chocolate mixture. Spread over the crust in the pan. Top with remaining crumbs. Refrigerate 6–8 hr. Serve cut in squares and top each with a dollop of whipped cream. Serves 6–8.

CHOCOLATE ALMOND PIE

   6   (1¼-oz) almond chocolate bars
1½ ounces unsweetened chocolate
1/4 cup milk
 20 marshmallows
   1 cup heavy cream, whipped
     9" crumb crust
     Garnish: 1/4 cup heavy cream, whipped

Combine almond chocolate bars, unsweetened chocolate, milk and marshmallows in top of double boiler. Heat until marshmallows are melted. Cool. Fold in whipped cream. Pile in crumb crust and refrigerate for about 4 hr. Serve cut in wedges and garnished with a dollop of whipped cream. Serves 6–8.

LEMON PIE

1/4 cup butter
  3 eggs, separated
  1 cup milk
1/4 cup lemon juice
  2 tbsp grated lemon peel
  1 cup sugar
  3 tbsp cornstarch
  1 cup sour cream
  1 9" baked pastry shell
1/2 cup heavy cream, whipped

Melt butter in saucepan. Beat in egg yolks and stir in milk, lemon juice, lemon peel, sugar and cornstarch. Cook, stirring constantly until filling is thickened. Remove from heat and cool. Fold in sour cream and pour into pastry shell. Chill at least 2 hr. Just before serving top with a thin frosting of whipped cream and garnish with a sprinkling of lemon rind. Meringue may be used instead of whipped cream. For meringue: beat the 3 egg whites until stiff, adding 1/4 tsp. of cream of tartar. Pile on cooled filling and bake at 325° for 10–15 min. or until meringue is golden. Then chill. Serves 8–10.

COFFEE MOUSSE

                32   marshmallows
                 1   cup strong coffee
                 2   cups heavy cream
                 2   tsp vanilla
                       Garnish: slivered almonds

Place marshmallows and coffee in top of double boiler. Heat until marshmallows have melted. Remove from heat and cool until mixture just begins to thicken. Whip cream with vanilla and fold in coffee mixture. Pour into sherbet glasses and refrigerate for 6–10 hr. Serve garnished with bits of toasted slivered almond. Serves 8.

LEMON SUNSHINE CAKE

                       CAKE

                 1   pkg Lemon Supreme cake mix
                 1   cup apricot nectar
                 4   eggs
               3/4   cup vegetable oil
                 1   pkg (3¾ oz) instant lemon pudding mix

                       GLAZE

                 2   lemons
              1¾   cup sifted confectioners' sugar

Preheat oven to 325°.
CAKE: combine cake mix and nectar. Add eggs, one at a time, beating after each addition. Blend in oil and pudding mix. Pour into a 3-qt. oiled and floured tube pan. Bake for 1 hr. Remove from oven and allow to stand for 20 min. before removing from pan.
GLAZE: grate lemon rind and juice the lemons. Combine rind and juice with confectioners' sugar and pour over warm cake. Allow cake to stand uncovered for 1 hr. or more before serving. Serves 10–12.

BUTTER BALLS

    1/2 cup butter, softened
      2 tbsp sugar
      1 cup sifted flour
      1 cup ground walnuts or pecans
      1 tsp vanilla
      1 tsp water
    1/2 cup sifted confectioners' sugar

Preheat oven to 300°.
Cream butter and sugar together. Add flour, nuts, vanilla and water. Mix thoroughly. Form into small balls and bake on un-greased cookie sheet for 30 min. Roll in confectioners' sugar while hot. Yield: about 30 cookies.

FRUIT-FILLED CREAM PUFFS

    3/4 cup water
    1/3 cup butter
    3/4 cup sifted flour
      3 eggs
    1/2 cup heavy cream, whipped
      3 tbsp sugar
    1½ cups cut-up fresh peaches or strawberries
         Garnish: confectioners' sugar

Preheat oven to 400°.
Bring water and butter to a rolling boil in a pan. Add flour all at once and stir vigorously over low heat until mixture forms a ball. Remove from heat and add eggs one at a time, beating by hand. Continue beating until mixture is smooth. Drop from a spoon into 6 mounds on an ungreased cookie sheet. Bake for about 45 min. Allow to cool slowly. To serve: cut off tops of puffs and scoop out any soft dough. Add sugar and fruit to whipped cream and fill each puff with fruit mixture. Replace tops and dust with sifted confectioners' sugar. Yield: 6 large puffs.

COCOA-FILLED ANGEL FOOD

1 angel-food cake

FILLING

3 cups heavy cream
1½ cups sifted confectioners' sugar
3/4 cup cocoa
1/4 tsp salt
2/3 cup chopped almonds, toasted

Slice top from angel food cake about 1" down from the top. Hollow out bottom portion, leaving wall about 1" thick on sides and bottom.
FILLING: combine cream, sugar, cocoa and salt in bowl. Whip until stiff. Divide mixture in half. Fold 1/3 cup almonds into half of the mixture. Use this to fill cake cavity. Replace top and ice top and sides with remaining cream mixture. Sprinkle with remaining almonds. Cover and refrigerate about 3 hr. or until set. Serves 12.

BERRIES WITH WINE SAUCE

1 pt strawberries
1 pt blueberries
1 pt raspberries
6 egg yolks
6 tbsp sugar
2/3 cup Marsala wine

Wash, hull and chill berries. Beat egg yolks, gradually adding sugar and wine. Cook over very low heat or over hot water, stirring with wire wisk until sauce foams and begins to thicken. Sauce may be kept warm over warm water or may be heated over very low heat before serving. If sauce becomes too thick, thin with a few drops of wine. Pour warm sauce over cold berries. Sauce may also be served cold. Serves 6.

COCONUT LEMON CHIFFON DESSERT

      1   tbsp unflavored gelatin
    1/2   cup cold water
    1/2   cup sugar
    1/8   tsp salt
      1   can (6-oz) frozen lemonade
      1   cup heavy cream, whipped
    1½   cups shredded coconut, toasted

Soften gelatin in cold water for 5 min. Add sugar and salt and place over low heat, stirring constantly until gelatin and sugar dissolve. Remove from heat and stir in undiluted lemonade concentrate. Chill until just beginning to set. Fold in whipped cream. Spoon alternating layers of lemon chiffon and coconut in sherbet glasses, finishing with coconut. Chill. Serves 6.

COFFEE CHANTILLY

    1½   tbsp unflavored gelatin
    3⅓   cups coffee
    1/2   cup sugar
      3   tbsp brandy
    1/4   tsp salt
      1   cup heavy cream, whipped
    1/2   cup chopped salted almonds, toasted
    1/3   cup sifted confectioners' sugar

Soften gelatin in 1/3 cup cold coffee for 5 min. Heat remaining 3 cups coffee to boiling. Add gelatin mixture and stir until dissolved. Remove from heat and add sugar, brandy and salt. Mix thoroughly. Pour into 8" square pan which has been rinsed with cold water. Chill until firm. To serve: cut gelatin into 1/2" cubes. Combine whipped cream, almonds and confectioners' sugar. Arrange gelatin and whipped cream in alternate layers in small individual serving dishes. Garnish with a cube of gelatin. Chill. Serves 6.

COFFEE-TOFFEE PIE

CRUST

1/2 pkg (10-oz) pie crust mix
1/4 cup light brown sugar, packed
3/4 cup finely chopped walnuts
1 ounce unsweetened chocolate, grated
1 tbsp water
1 tsp vanilla

FILLING

1/2 cup butter, softened
3/4 cup sugar
1 ounce unsweetened chocolate, melted
1 tbsp instant coffee
2 eggs

TOPPING

2 cups heavy cream, whipped
2 tbsp instant coffee
1/3 cup sifted confectioners' sugar
     Garnish: chocolate curls

Preheat oven to 375°.
CRUST: combine pie crust mix, sugar, walnuts and grated chocolate. Mix in water and vanilla. Pat mixture into 9" pie plate and bake 15 min. Cool.
FILLING: cream butter with sugar until fluffy. Add melted chocolate and 1 tbsp. coffee. Add eggs one at a time, beating very well after each addition. Pour in pie shell. Chill overnight.
TOPPING: combine whipped cream, 2 tbsp. coffee and confectioners' sugar. Pile on pie to cover. Garnish with chocolate curls.
Serves 6–8.

FUDGE PUDDING CAKE

1	cup sifted flour
2	tsp baking powder
1/4	tsp salt
3/4	cup sugar
2	tbsp plus 1/4 cup cocoa
1/2	cup milk
2	tbsp butter, melted
3/4	cup chopped walnuts
1	cup light brown sugar, packed
1/2	tsp cinnamon
2	cups hot water
	Garnish: whipped cream

Preheat oven to 350°.
Sift flour, baking powder, salt, sugar and 2 tbsp. cocoa together. Stir in milk and butter. Fold in nuts. Spread in 9" square pan. Sprinkle with mixture of brown sugar and 1/4 cup cocoa and cinnamon. Pour water over all. Bake for about 45 min. Cake will rise to top and sauce will remain on bottom of pan. Serve warm cut in squares and inverted on dessert plate. Spoon sauce over pieces. Garnish with a dollop of whipped cream. Serves 8–10.

ELEGANT GRAPES

1½	lbs seedless green grapes
1/2	cup honey
4	tbsp cognac or brandy
4	tbsp lemon juice
2	cups sour cream
2	tbsp brown sugar

Wash grapes. Mix honey, cognac and lemon juice. Pour over grapes. Mix well and refrigerate overnight. Serve in individual dessert dishes and top with 1/3 cup sour cream sprinkled with 1 tsp. brown sugar. Serves 6.

COLD FUDGE SOUFFLÉ

  1   tbsp unflavored gelatin
1/2   cup cold water
1/2   cup boiling water
  5   ounces unsweetened chocolate
  1   cup milk
  5   eggs, separated
  1   cup sugar
  1   tsp vanilla

TOPPING

  1   cup heavy cream
  2   tsp sugar
1½   tsp vanilla
      Garnish: chocolate curls

Soften gelatin in cold water for 5 min. Add boiling water and stir until gelatin is dissolved. Melt chocolate in milk over hot water or very low heat. Cool. Beat egg yolks with sugar until fluffy. Thoroughly combine the gelatin, melted chocolate, sugar mixture, and vanilla. Beat egg whites until stiff and fold into the chocolate mixture. Pour into a 1½-qt. soufflé dish or individual sherbert glasses. Chill 3 or 4 hr. To serve: whip the cream with sugar and vanilla and pile on top of soufflé. Serve garnished with chocolate curls. Serves 6–8.

FROZEN GINGER ROLL

  1   pkg (14½-oz) gingerbread mix
  1   egg
1½   cups confectioners' sugar
  2   cups heavy cream, whipped
      or lemon sherbert or maple walnut ice cream

Prepare gingerbread according to package directions, adding an egg to the liquid. Grease a 10½" x 15½" jelly roll pan. Line the bottom with wax paper and grease the paper. Spread batter evenly over pan and bake for about 12 min. or until cake springs back when gently pressed with finger. While the cake is baking, sift 1¼ cups confectioners' sugar onto a clean towel. Remove cake from oven and immediately turn onto sugar. Peel away wax paper. Roll warm cake up in towel, jelly roll fashion. Place seam side down and allow to cool.

Unroll cake and spread with whipped cream, softened sherbert or ice cream. Reroll cake and wrap in foil. Freeze until serving time. To serve: sift remaining 1/4 cup confectioners' sugar on top and slice. Serves 6–8.

HAWAIIAN POUND CAKE

1	lb butter, softened
2	cups sugar
2	cups sifted flour
6	eggs
1½	tsp vanilla
2	cans (3½-oz.) shredded coconut

GLAZE

1	cup sugar
1/2	cup water
2	tsp coconut liqueur or almond extract

Preheat oven to 350°.

Cream the butter with sugar until fluffy. Add 1 cup of flour and mix thoroughly. Add eggs, one at a time, beating well after each addition. Add vanilla. Mix the remaining flour with the coconut and add it to the batter. Pour batter into a greased 9" tube pan. Bake for about 1 hr. and 15 min. or until a toothpick inserted into the cake comes out clean. Turn out of pan and glaze.

GLAZE: combine ingredients and simmer for 10 min. Brush top of hot cake with glaze and allow to drip down the sides. Cool. Cake is best when allowed to sit 24 hr. for flavors to blend. Serves 16–18.

DESSERT TARTS

PASTRY

2	cups sifted flour
1	tsp salt
1/3	cup butter
1/3	cup shortening
4–5	tbsp water

Preheat oven to 425°.

Sift flour with salt. With two knives cut in butter until consistency of coarse meal. Cut in shortening until it is the size of large peas. Sprinkle water on flour mixture, a tablespoon at a time, only until mixture is moist. Press dough together into a ball. Divide into 6 equal parts. Roll each piece into a 4″ pastry round. Fit over backs of muffin cups or custard cups, making pleats so pastry will fit. Prick pastry with a fork. Place cups on a cookie sheet and bake 8–10 min. Cool. Remove from cups. Yield: 6 tart shells.

GLAZED FRUIT FILLING

1	pkg (3-oz) cream cheese, softened
2–3	tbsp orange juice
3	cups fresh or frozen fruit (berries, peaches)
3/4	cup currant jelly, melted

Combine cream cheese with juice and beat until creamy. Line each tart shell with some of the cheese. Fill with fruit and top each with 2 tbsp. of melted jelly. Chill. Yield: 6 tarts.

ICE CREAM FILLING

1½	pts ice cream
3–4	cups fudge or butterscotch sauce
	or fresh or frozen fruit
	or nuts, shaved chocolate or shredded coconut

Fill cooled tart shells with ice cream. Top with a sauce or another topping. Wrap in foil and freeze. Yield: 6 tarts.

COCONUT FILLING

3/4 cup sugar
1 tbsp plus 2 tsp cornstarch
1/2 tsp salt
3/4 cup milk
2 egg yolks, beaten
3 tbsp butter
3/4 tsp vanilla
3/4 cup shredded coconut
1/4 cup shredded coconut, toasted

Mix sugar, cornstarch and salt in saucepan. Gradually add milk, stirring until smooth. Cook and stir over low heat until mixture boils. Boil 1 min. Remove from heat and stir half the mixture into the beaten egg yolks. Beat egg mixture back into remaining sauce in pan. Stir in butter, vanilla and shredded coconut. Pour into cooled tart shells. Sprinkle with toasted coconut. Chill. Yield: 6 tarts.

CHOCOLATE MERINGUE COOKIES

2 egg whites
3/4 cup sugar
1 pkg (6-oz) chocolate bits
1/2 tsp vanilla

Preheat oven to 350°.
Beat egg whites until stiff, gradually adding sugar. Add chocolate bits and vanilla. Arrange by teaspoonful on wax paper on a cookie sheet. Place cookies in 350° oven and turn off heat. Leave in oven 6 hr. or overnight. Yield: about 30 cookies.
SPICE MERINGUE: mix together 2 tsp. cinnamon, 1/4 tsp. nutmeg and 1/4 tsp. ground cloves. Add to the stiffly beaten egg whites instead of the chocolate.
NUT MERINGUE: mix 1 cup finely ground walnuts or pecans with the egg white mixture instead of the chocolate.

ICE CREAM BALLS

PEANUT BUTTER

1	cup graham cracker crumbs
1/4	cup chunky peanut butter
2	tbsp sugar
1/2	tsp cinnamon
1	qt vanilla ice cream
	chocolate sauce

Combine crumbs, peanut butter, sugar and cinnamon. Make 8 large ice cream balls. Roll in crumb mixture. Freeze until ready to serve. Serve with hot or cold chocolate sauce. Serves 8.

PECAN

1	qt butter pecan ice cream
1½	cups finely chopped pecans
	butterscotch sauce

COCONUT

1	qt vanilla ice cream
1½	cups shredded coconut
	chocolate sauce

Make 8 large ice cream balls. Roll in pecans *or* coconut. Freeze until ready to serve. Serve with hot or cold sauce. Serves 8.

SUGARED PECANS

2	egg whites
1	cup sugar
1/4	cup butter, melted
1	lb shelled pecans, halved

Preheat oven to 300°.
Beat egg whites until stiff. Stir in sugar and butter. Add pecans and mix until coated. Spread on a greased cookie sheet. Bake for about 45 min. or until dry, turning every 15 min. with a spatula. Yield: 1 lb. nuts.

BAKED ORANGE ALASKA

   3   navel oranges
   1   small pineapple, peeled
1/2 lb seedless green grapes
1½ tbsp crystallized ginger
1/4 cup sugar
   3   egg whites
1/4 cup honey
   3   tbsp chopped almonds, toasted
      GARNISH: fresh mint leaves

Preheat oven to 450°.
Cut oranges in half and remove fruit. Set aside orange shells. Chop the pineapple, and orange and halve the grapes. Combine fruit with 1 tbsp. of ginger and sugar and spoon into orange shells. Beat the egg whites until stiff, gradually blending in honey. Pile on top of orange shells, being sure to spread it to the edges. Sprinkle meringue with almonds and the remaining ginger. Bake for 5 min. until brown. Cool and then chill in refrigerator. Garnish with mint leaves. Serves 6.

FROSTED ORANGE

   6   navel oranges
   2   egg whites
   1   cup sugar
   3   cups assorted melon balls (cantaloupe, honeydew, watermelon)
      Garnish: fresh mint leaves

Cut tops off oranges. Scoop out the pulp. Cut a thin slice off the bottom of the orange so that it will stand upright. Do *not* cut through shell. Brush the oranges and their tops with unbeaten egg white. Chill for about 1/2 hr. Roll oranges and tops in sugar. Fill oranges with assorted melon balls and partially replace the tops, allowing some of the melon balls to show. Chill. Serve garnished with mint, both in cup and on plate. Serve very cold. Serves 6.

LEMON SNOW

3/4 cup sugar
1 tbsp unflavored gelatin
1¼ cups water
1/4 cup lemon juice
1 tbsp grated lemon rind
2 egg whites
Garnish: lemon

CUSTARD SAUCE

1/4 cup sugar
1 tbsp cornstarch
2 egg yolks
2 cups milk
1 tbsp butter
1½ tsp vanilla

Combine sugar, gelatin and water and bring to a boil, stirring constantly. Add lemon juice and lemon rind. Cool until mixture is just beginning to set. Beat egg whites until stiff. Slowly blend gelatin into egg whites. Continue stirring until mixture is very well blended and no gelatin remains at the bottom. Pour into a dessert bowl or individual dessert dishes. Chill.

CUSTARD SAUCE: mix sugar with cornstarch in pan. Add egg yolks and mix thoroughly. Stir milk in gradually. Bring to a boil, stirring constantly. Boil 1 min. Add butter and vanilla. Mix well and chill.

To serve: top with custard sauce and garnish with a thin slice of lemon. Serves 6.

LEMON SQUARES

CRUST

1 cup sifted flour
1/4 cup confectioners' sugar
1/4 cup butter, melted

152   *DESSERTS*

FILLING

        1   cup sugar
        2   tbsp flour
      1/2   tsp baking powder
        2   eggs, beaten
        3   tbsp lemon juice
      1/2   tsp lemon extract
             confectioners' sugar

Preheat oven to 350°.
CRUST: combine 1 cup flour, confectioners' sugar and butter.
Press dough in the bottom of a greased 8" square pan. Bake for
20 min.
FILLING: combine 1 cup sugar, 2 tbsp. flour and baking powder.
Add eggs, lemon juice and lemon extract, beating until fluffy.
Spread evenly over baked crust. Bake for 25 min. Cut into squares
while still warm and dust with sifted confectioners' sugar. Yield:
16 squares.

MOCHA NUT BALLS

        1   cup butter, softened
      1/2   cup sugar
        1   tsp almond extract
        2   tsp instant coffee
      1/4   cup cocoa
      1/2   tsp salt
      1¾   cups sifted flour
        2   cups finely chopped pecans
        1   cup sifted confectioners' sugar

Preheat oven to 325°.
Cream butter, sugar and almond extract together until fluffy. Add
coffee, cocoa, salt and flour. Mix thoroughly. Add nuts. Shape
into 1" balls and bake on an ungreased cookie sheet for 15 min.
Cool and roll in confectioners' sugar. Yield: about 60 balls.

ORANGE SPONGE PUDDING

        1/2   cup sugar
        4½   tbsp flour
        1   can (11-oz) mandarin oranges
        2   tbsp grated orange rind
        4   eggs, separated
        3/4   cup milk
        2   tbsp orange juice
        2   tbsp butter, melted

Preheat oven to 350°.

Combine sugar, flour, 3/4 cup syrup from the oranges, orange rind, egg yolks, milk, orange juice and butter. Beat the egg whites until stiff and fold into the orange mixture. Pour mixture into 6 buttered 3½" custard cups. Place the dishes in a pan that contains 1" of hot water. Bake for 45 min. or until a knife inserted in pudding comes out clean. Run a knife around the edge to loosen pudding. Unmold on plates. Garnish with mint leaves and the mandarin oranges. May be served hot or cold. Serves 6.

MARBLED CREAM CHEESE BROWNIES

        4   ounces sweet chocolate
        5   tbsp butter, softened
        4   ounces cream cheese, softened
        1   cup sugar
        3   eggs
        1   tbsp plus 1/2 cup flour
        1/2   tsp lemon juice
        1½   tsp vanilla
        1/2   tsp baking powder
        1/4   tsp salt
        1/2   cup chopped walnuts
        1/2   tsp almond extract

Preheat oven to 350°.
Melt chocolate with 3 tbsp. of the butter over low heat. Cool.

Cream remaining 2 tbsp. of butter with cream cheese and 1/4 cup sugar until fluffy. Beat in 1 egg, 1 tbsp. flour, lemon juice and 1/2 tsp. vanilla. Set aside.

In another bowl beat remaining 2 eggs until fluffy. Gradually beat in remaining 3/4 cup sugar and beat until thick. Mix together baking powder, salt and remaining 1/2 cup of flour and fold into beaten egg mixture. Add chocolate, nuts, almond extract and remaining 1 tsp. vanilla, mixing until well blended. Spread all but 1 cup on the chocolate mixture in a greased 9" square pan. Top with cheese mixture. Then spoon remaining chocolate over cheese and swirl through batter with a knife to produce marbled effect. Bake for 30 min. or until a toothpick inserted into the brownies comes out clean. Cool. Cut in squares. Yield: 16–20 squares.

PUMPKIN CHIFFON PIE

1	tbsp unflavored gelatin
2/3	cup light brown sugar, packed
1/2	tsp salt
3/4	tsp cinnamon
1/2	tsp nutmeg
1/2	tsp ginger
1	can (16-oz) pumpkin
3	eggs, separated
1/2	cup milk
1/2	cup sugar
	9" crumb crust
1/2	cup heavy cream, whipped

In a saucepan, combine gelatin, brown sugar, salt, cinnamon, nutmeg, ginger, pumpkin, egg yolks and milk. Mix thoroughly. Cook over medium heat, stirring constantly until the mixture boils. Remove from heat and cool until it begins to set. Beat egg whites until stiff, gradually adding 1/2 cup sugar. Fold pumpkin mixture into the egg whites. Pile into crust. Chill until set. Serve cut in wedges and topped with whipped cream sprinkled with cinnamon. Serves 6–8.

EGGNOG CHIFFON PIE

      1   tbsp unflavored gelatin
      2   tbsp cold water
      3   eggs, separated
  1/2   cup sugar
          dash of salt
  1/4   tsp nutmeg
  2/3   cup light cream, scalded
      2   tbsp dark rum
  1½   tsp vanilla
  1/2   cup heavy cream, whipped
      1   8" crumb crust
          Garnish: whipped cream

Soften gelatin in cold water for 5 min. Beat egg yolks with 1/4 cup of sugar, salt and nutmeg. Stir into scalded cream. Heat, stirring constantly until mixture thickens. Add gelatin and stir until dissolved. Remove from heat, add rum and vanilla. Chill until mixture is just beginning to set. Beat egg whites until stiff, gradually adding the remaining 1/4 cup sugar. Fold into gelatin mixture. Fold in whipped cream. Pile into prepared crumb crust. Chill until set. Serve garnished with a dollop of whipped cream and a sprinkle of nutmeg. Serves 6–8.

MOCHA-NUT PIE

          CRUST

  1½   cups chocolate cookie crumbs
      2   tbsp sugar
  1/4   tsp cinnamon
  1/3   cup butter, melted
  1/2   cup finely chopped almonds

          FILLING

      3   egg yolks
  1½   cups light cream

        1   tbsp unflavored gelatin
     1/2   cup sugar
     1/4   tsp salt
     1½   tbsp instant coffee
        2   tbsp brandy
     3/4   cup heavy cream, whipped
     1/2   cup chopped almonds
              Garnish: chocolate curls

CRUST: combine cookie crumbs, sugar, cinnamon, butter and almonds. Press mixture against bottom and sides of a 9" pie plate.
Chill.
FILLING: beat egg yolks and cream together until well blended.
Combine gelatin, sugar, salt and coffee in a large saucepan. Add
egg yolk mixture and cook over low heat, stirring constantly until
mixture thickens. Remove from heat and stir in brandy. Chill for
about 1 hr. Fold in whipped cream and almonds. Pile into prepared crust. Chill 4 hr. Garnish with almonds and chocolate curls.
Serves 6–8.

PECAN PIE

        3   eggs, beaten
        1   box (1-lb) light brown sugar
     1/4   lb butter, melted
        1   tsp vanilla
              dash of salt
     3/4   cup broken pecans
              9" pie shell

Preheat oven to 375°.
Thoroughly combine all the ingredients. Pour into pie shell and
bake at 375° for 10 min. for crust to brown. Reduce oven temperature to 325° and bake for 40 min. Pie should be beginning to set
when removed from oven. It will completely set when cooled.
May be served with a dollop of whipped cream or vanilla ice
cream. Serves 8.

GLAZED STRAWBERRIES

1   qt fresh strawberries
1/4   cup raspberry jam
2   tbsp sugar
1/4   cup water
2   tbsp Kirsch
1/4   cup slivered almonds

Wash, hull and chill berries. Combine the jam, sugar and water and bring to a boil. Add Kirsch and chill. Pile berries in individual dessert dishes and pour sauce over them. Sprinkle with almonds. Serves 6.

NUT-CRUMB TORTE

1   cup butter, softened
1   cup sugar
1   tsp cinnamon
1   tbsp vanilla
4   eggs
3   cups fine graham cracker crumbs
1   cup ground walnuts or pecans
1   tbsp baking powder
1   cup milk

CHOCOLATE FROSTING

1   pkg (6-oz) chocolate bits
1/4   cup water
1½   tsp instant coffee
1/4   cup sugar
2   eggs beaten
1/2   cup butter

Preheat oven to 350°.
Cream butter with sugar until fluffy. Add cinnamon, vanilla and eggs, one at a time, beating after each addition. Combine crumbs, nuts, baking powder. Add to butter mixture alternating with milk.

Pour into three greased 8" cake pans. Bake for 30 min. Turn out on rack to cool.

CHOCOLATE FROSTING: combine chocolate, water, coffee and sugar. Heat very slowly until melted. Pour half the hot chocolate mixture into the beaten eggs, stirring constantly. Return egg mixture to pan. Add butter, gradually stirring until melted. Chill until spreading consistency.

Put layers together with chocolate frosting and cut into wedges. Serves 10–12.

ORANGE SQUARES

CRUST

1/4	cup butter, softened
1	cup sifted flour

FILLING

2	eggs, beaten
1	cup light brown sugar, packed
1	tsp baking powder
1	cup shredded coconut
1/2	cup chopped walnuts

FROSTING

2	tbsp butter, melted
1	cup confectioners' sugar
	rind of 1 orange, grated
	orange juice

Preheat oven to 350°.

CRUST: combine butter with flour until crumbly. Pat into a greased 9" square pan. Bake 12 min.

FILLING: combine eggs, brown sugar, baking powder, coconut and walnuts. Spread over baked crust. Bake 30 min. Cool.

FROSTING: combine melted butter, confectioners' sugar, orange rind and enough orange juice to attain a spreading consistency. Spread frosting to cover. Cut into squares. Yield: 16 squares.

ORANGE COCONUT MOUSSE

       1   egg white
    1/2   cup sugar
       1   cup heavy cream
            dash of salt
       1   tsp grated orange rind
    1/4   cup shredded coconut, toasted

Beat egg whites until stiff, gradually adding sugar. Whip the cream and fold into egg whites. Fold in remaining ingredients. Spoon the mousse into small paper tortoni cups. Serve garnished with additional toasted coconut. Chill thoroughly or freeze before serving. Serves 8–10.

BRANDIED PEACH WITH VANILLA SAUCE

    2½   cups water
    1¼   cups sugar
       1   vanilla bean
       6   medium ripe peaches
    1/2   cup brandy

            VANILLA SAUCE

    1/3   cup confectioners' sugar
    1/4   cup butter
    1/2   cup heavy cream
       2   tsp vanilla

Combine water, sugar and vanilla bean and bring to a boil. Simmer for 10 min. Add peaches and simmer, turning occasionally until just tender. Cool in syrup and remove vanilla bean. Peel, halve and pit the cooled peaches. Add brandy to syrup and simmer for 10 min. Return the peaches to the syrup and chill.
VANILLA SAUCE: combine sugar and butter in pan. Cook, stirring, over low heat until thickened and smooth. Cool. Whip cream with the vanilla and fold into the sauce. To serve: place chilled peaches in sherbet glasses and top with sauce. Serves 6.

POUND CAKE

       2 cups sifted cake flour
    1/2 tsp salt
       1 tsp baking powder
    1/2 lb butter, softened
    1½ cups sugar
       4 eggs
    1/2 cup milk
    1½ tsp vanilla
       1 tbsp brandy

Preheat oven to 350°.
Sift flour, salt and baking powder together. Set aside. Cream butter with sugar until fluffy. Add eggs, one at a time, beating well after each addition. Combine milk and flavorings. Add to egg mixture, alternating with flour mixture. Stir only until blended. Grease a 9" x 5" loaf pan. Place a piece of foil in pan so that it covers bottom and projects over the sides of the pan. Pour in batter and bake for 1 hr. or until a toothpick inserted in the cake comes out clean. Serve plain or with fresh fruit or ice cream. Yield: 1 cake.

PEACH MACAROON FREEZE

       2 cups mashed fresh peaches
       1 cup sugar
       1 tbsp lemon juice
       1 cup heavy cream
       2 tsp Grand Marnier
       1 cup coarse macaroon crumbs
           Garnish: peach

Combine peaches with sugar and lemon juice. Whip cream with the Grand Marnier and fold into the peach mixture. Cover bottom of a 1-qt. freezer tray with half of the crumbs. Pour peach mixture on top. Sprinkle remaining crumbs over the top and freeze for 6 hr. Cut into squares or slices and serve immediately, garnished with fresh peach slices. Serves 6–8.

STRAWBERRY BAVARIAN CREAM

Blender

         2   tbsp unflavored gelatin
       1/4   cup cold milk
         1   pkg (10-oz) frozen strawberries, thawed
       1/4   cup sugar
         2   egg yolks
         1   cup heavy cream
         1   cup crushed ice
              Garnish: strawberries

Soften gelatin in milk for 5 min. Drain strawberries, reserving 1/2 cup juice. Heat juice until just simmering. Pour into blender. Add the gelatin and blend until smooth. Add sugar, strawberries and egg yolks. Cover and blend about 10 sec. Leaving the motor on, remove the cover and add cream and crushed ice. Blend until it just begins to thicken. Pour into a 4-cup mold or special serving dish. Chill until set about 3 hr. Garnish with strawberries. Serves 6.

SHERRY-ALMOND CHIFFON PIE

         1   tbsp unflavored gelatin
       1/4   cup cold water
         1   cup milk
       1/2   cup sugar
       1/2   tsp salt
         3   eggs, separated
       1/2   cup heavy cream, whipped
         3   tbsp dry sherry
         1   tsp vanilla
       1/2   cup chopped almonds, toasted
         1   9" baked pie shell
              Garnish: chocolate curls

Soften gelatin in cold water for 5 min. Combine milk, 1/4 cup sugar and salt. Heat, stirring until the milk is scalded. Beat egg yolks and stir in half the hot milk mixture. Return to saucepan and cook, stirring until slightly thickened. Blend in softened gelatin and stir until dissolved. Chill until mixture is just beginning to set. Beat egg whites until stiff, gradually adding remaining 1/4 cup sugar. Fold egg whites and whipped cream into chilled custard. Add sherry, vanilla and nuts. Pile into baked pie shell. Chill until firm. Garnish with grated chocolate curls. Serves 8.

PRUNE WHIP

2	tbsp sugar
1½	cups heavy cream
1	tsp lemon juice
3	jars (3¾-oz) baby prunes
	Garnish: dried prunes

Whip sugar with cream. Mix lemon juice into prunes and fold into whipped cream. Pour into sherbet glasses. Garnish with a small slice of dried prune on top of each. Serves 6.

RUM DEVIL'S FOOD CAKE

1	Devil's Food Cake mix
1	cup light rum
1/2	cup light corn syrup
1	cup heavy cream, whipped
	Garnish: chocolate curls

Preheat oven to 350°.
Make cake according to package directions, but pour into a greased tube pan and bake for 45 min., or until toothpick inserted into cake comes out clean. Remove from oven and allow to stand for 5 min. Combine rum and corn syrup and pour half the mixture over the cake. Allow to stand for 15 min. Turn cake onto a platter. Pour the remaining rum mixture over the cake. Cool thoroughly. Cover with whipped cream and garnish with chocolate curls. Serves 10–12.

CREAM VELVET FREEZE

      1/2   cup sugar
        2   tbsp water
        2   egg yolks
            dash of salt
        2   tbsp cognac
      1½   cups heavy cream, whipped
      1/4   cup finely chopped almonds
            Garnish: unsweetened chocolate

Combine sugar and water and bring to a boil. Cook until syrup forms a soft ball when a drop is put in a glass of cold water, or until syrup registers 236° on a candy thermometer. Beat egg yolks with the salt until they are very thick. Add syrup very gradually while beating and continue beating until mixture forms peaks, or about 5 min. Chill. Add cognac and fold in whipped cream and almonds. Spoon mixture into 1/2-cup molds or small paper dessert cups. Garnish with grated unsweetened chocolate. Cover and freeze. Note: this tends to get icy if kept too long. Best made night before or early morning of party. Serves 6–8.
CHOCOLATE VELVET: omit nuts and add 3 tbsp. of cocoa to sugar and water.
COFFEE VELVET: omit nuts and add 2 tsp. instant coffee to sugar and water.

STRAWBERRY MERINGUE

        3   egg whites
      1/4   tsp cream of tartar
        1   cup sugar
        1   pt strawberries
        1   tbsp Kirsch
      1½   cups heavy cream, whipped
            Garnish: mint leaves

Preheat oven to 275°.
Beat egg whites until stiff and glossy, gradually adding cream of

tartar and sugar. Place a greased sheet of aluminum foil on a cookie sheet. Spread meringue on foil and shape to form an 11″ shell. Bake for 1½ hr. Then turn oven off and leave meringue in oven for at least another 2 hr. Wash, hull and slice strawberries, putting aside 4 or 5 for garnish. Fold strawberries into whipped cream. Heap into meringue shell. Chill for about 2 hr. Garnish with sliced strawberries and mint leaves. Serves 6–8.

GREEK WALNUT TORTE

13	filo pastry sheets (see directions p. 87)
1/4	lb butter, melted, plus 1/4 cup, softened
1/2	cup sugar
1¼	lbs chopped walnuts

SYRUP

1	cup sugar
1	cup water
1/2	lemon
3/4	cup honey
1	stick cinnamon

Preheat oven to 250°.
Lightly butter a 8″ x 12″ shallow baking dish. Cover bottom and sides of baking dish with a whole filo sheet and brush with butter. Layer 4 more filo sheets into the dish, brushing each layer with butter. Cover with an unbuttered sheet. Mix remaining butter, sugar and walnuts together. Spread half the walnut mixture to cover filo. Add an unbuttered filo sheet and spread the remaining walnut mixture. Cover with 6 remaining filo sheets, brushing each with butter. Turn down filo sides to seal. Brush top with butter. Score pastry in diamond shaped pieces. Do not cut through bottom layer. Bake for 1 hr. or until crisp and golden. Remove from oven and cool.
SYRUP: combine sugar, water and lemon and bring to a boil. Boil 5 min. Remove lemon and add honey and cinnamon. Boil 5 min. longer. Remove cinnamon stick. Pour over cooled torte. Serves 8–10.

PEACH CREAM

6 whole fresh peaches
1 cup dry sherry
1 cup port wine
2 tbsp sugar
2 tbsp red currant jelly
   vanilla ice cream

Peel, halve, and pit peaches. Heat wines with sugar. Add peaches. Simmer about 20 min. turning occasionally. Chill. Add jelly to wine mixture and continue cooking until it is a thick syrup. To serve: fill each peach half with ice cream and pour hot syrup over the top. Serves 6.

Equivalents and Substitutions

dash	= less than 1/8 tsp
1 tbsp	= 3 tsp
4 tbsp	= ¼ cup
5⅓ tbsp	= ⅓ cup
8 tbsp	= ½ cup
2 tbsp	= 1/8 cup or 1 fluid oz
1 cup	= 8 oz
1 cup	= ½ pt
2 cups	= 1 pt
1 qt	= 4 cups or 2 pt
2 sticks butter	= ½ lb or 1 cup
¼ lb grated cheese	= 1 cup
1 lb cheese	= 5 cups grated or 4 cups dry grated
8-oz cream cheese	= 1 cup
1 lemon	= 2–3 tbsp juice and 2 tsp rind
1 orange	= ½ cup juice and 2–3 tbsp rind
1 lb flour	= 4 cups sifted
½ lb sliced fresh mushrooms	= 2½ cups
1 lb sliced fresh mushrooms	= 8-oz can
1 lb ground cooked meat	= 3 cups
1 lb crabmeat	= 2 cups
¼–½ tsp dried herbs	= 1 tbsp fresh
1/8 tsp garlic powder	= 1 small clove
1 lb walnuts	= 3½ cups
1 can (3½-oz) shredded coconut	= 1 1/3 cups
1 lb sugar	= 2 cups
1 square chocolate	= 1 oz
1 pt heavy cream	= 4 cups, whipped

167

Index

I N D E X   173

Seafood *(continued)*
  soup
    clam bisque, *12*
    crab bisque, *10*
    crabmeat, *17*
    tuna bisque, *11*
    tuna fish Indienne, *73*
    tuna fish loaf, baked, *73*
Sesame bread, *24*
Sesame seed sticks, *35*
Sherry-almond chiffon pie, *162*
Shrimp and avocado salad, *115*
Shrimp and cheese, molded, *58*
Shrimp and crab salad, *58*
Shrimp-chick pea salad, *113*
Shrimp, Far East, *60*
Shrimp jambalaya, *55*
Shrimp mold, *61*
Shrimp Newburg, easy, *60*
Shrimp New Orleans, *57*
Shrimp strudel, *59*
Shrimp with Béarnaise, *61*
Soufflés
  cheese and shrimp, *56*
  cheese, *42*
  chicken, *78*
  crabmeat-ham-chicken, *67*
  sour cream, *40*
  tuna fish ring, *74*
Soups, cold
  avocado, *2*
  blueberry, *3*
  borscht, quick, *3*
  carrot Vichyssoise, *4*
  chicken, curried, *5*
  clam bisque, *12*
  crab bisque, *10*
  Florida, *14*
  gazpacho #1, *6*
  gazpacho #2, *6*
  lima bean, cream of, *4*
  parsley, *17*
  sour cream tomato, *9*
  spinach, *8*
  tarragon broth, jellied, *5*
  tomato cream, fresh, *8*
  Vichyssoise, *7*
Soups, hot
  almond, *15*
  asparagus, curried, *15*
  crab bisque, *10*
  crabmeat, *17*
  cream of
    cauliflower, *11*
    green bean, *13*
    water cress, *16*
  egg and lemon, *18*
  mushroom, clear, *10*

Soups *(continued)*
  mushroom, fresh, *16*
  onion, *12*
  parsley, *17*
  peanut, Williamsburg, *13*
  pimiento-cheese, *18*
  pumpkin, *14*
  tomato juice, *9*
  tuna bisque, *11*
Sour cream and chive biscuits, *36*
Sour cream dressing, *124*
Sour cream soufflé, *40*
Sour cream tomato soup, *9*
Spice dressing, *119*
Spice bread, *27*
Spinach salad, *113*
Spinach soup, chilled, *8*
Strawberries, glazed, *158*
Strawberry Bavarian cream, *162*
Strawberry meringue, *164*
Strawberry sour cream mold, *115*

Table
  equivalents and substitutions, *167*
Tarts, *see* Desserts
Tarragon broth, jellied, *5*
Tarragon salad dressing, *122*
Tomato and rice salad, fresh, *110*
Tomato, aspic carousel, *84*
Tomato cream soup, fresh, *8*
Tomato juice soup, *9*
Tomato quiche, *54*
Tomato salad, molded, *114*
Tortes, *see* Desserts
Tuna bisque, *11*
Tuna fish Indienne, *73*
Tuna fish loaf, baked, *73*
Tuna fish soufflé ring, *79*
Tuna fish spaghetti salad, *71*
Turkey and cheese sandwiches, *83*

Vanilla sauce, *160*
Veal and ham rolls, *89*
Vegetable mold, garden, *117*
Vegetable salads, *see* Salads
Vegetable sour cream mold, fresh, *114*
Vichyssoise, *7*

Waldorf salad mold, *105*
Walnut torte, Greek, *165*
Water cress soup, cream of, *16*
Watermelon basket, *84*
Welsh rarebit, *41*
Western dressing, *122*
Western salad, *116*
Wild rice mold with shrimp, *57*
Wine dressing, *124*
Wine sauce, *80*